Drupal Multimedia

Create media-rich Drupal sites by learning to embed
and manipulate images, video, and audio

Aaron Winborn

BIRMINGHAM - MUMBAI

Drupal Multimedia

First published:October 2008

Production Reference: 1141008

Published by Packt Publishing Ltd.
32 Lincoln Road
Olton
Birmingham, B27 6PA, UK.

ISBN 978-1-847194-60-2

www.packtpub.com

Cover Image by Vinayak Chittar (vinayak.chittar@gmail.com)

Credits

Autrhor

Aaron Winborn

Reviewers

James Walker

Kristof De Jaeger

Bruno De Bondt

Ryan Shrout

Senior Acquisition Editor

Douglas Paterson

Development Editor

Swapna V. Verlekar

Technical Editor

Abhinav Prasoon

Copy Editor

Sneha Kulkarni

Editorial Team Leader

Mithil Kulkarni

Project Manager

Abhijeet Deobhakta

Project Coordinator

Lata Basantani

Indexer

Rekha Nair

Proofreader

Chris Smith

Production Coordinator

Aparna Bhagat

Cover Work

Aparna Bhagat

About the Author

Aaron Winborn has been a Drupal developer for over three years, most of that time for Advomatic, where he has helped to develop excellent sites for such companies and organizations as Air America, Sony, NRDC, and Mozilla. Before that, he had followed dual passions for teaching and web development for nearly a decade, teaching at a Sudbury school (a democratic and age-mixed model for young people).

He has contributed several modules to the Drupal community, such as Embedded Media Field, jQuery Media, Views Slideshow, and the upcoming Drupal Media Player. He has also been active in core development, most recently advocating and contributing to efforts for better media support in Drupal 7, such as the hook_file patch and a centralized jQuery plug-in/library registry. As a panelist at several conferences, such as DrupalCon Boston, DrupalCampNYC, and DrupalCampDenver, Aaron continues to share his experience with using multimedia in Drupal with the community.

Aaron has always been interested in teaching and writing. Prior to his current employment with Advomatic, he taught at a Sudbury model school, in a diverse range of classes such as Computer Game Design, Silk-screening, and a History of the Vietnam War. He was also puppeteer for two puppet theaters.

Aaron lives with his partner Gwen and their daughter Ashlin in Harrisburg, Pennsylvania. Theo, their cat, rules the house, while their dog, Mia, sneakily sleeps on their couch when they're out. You can read about Aaron's ongoing adventures with Drupal at `AaronWinborn.com`, and visit this book's companion site at `DrupalMultimedia.org`.

Drupal Multimedia could not have been written without the support and encouragement of the great folks at Advomatic, particularly Adam Mordecai, who helped me start running with Drupal; Aaron Welch, who has single-handedly wrestled our servers when needed, and has built an impeccable support team so he doesn't need to; Dylan Clear, who must have been a juggler in another life; Sam Tresler, his simple practicality and clear values dearly appreciated by me; Marco Carbone, who has helped me dig myself out of coding trouble on several occasions; Jack Haas, whose theming wizardry is always appreciated; Fred Gooltz, whose particular vision has inspired at least of couple of modules from me; and Liz Morton, who makes sure we pay the piper's dues.

I also want to thank the numerous people in the larger Drupal community who have helped me. Dries Buytaert, without whose original vision we would have all been stuck hacking away at some second-rate solution. Neil Drumm, who is a wizard at high-performance queries, and can cook a mean vegan dinner. Morbus Iff, who can take a hundred lines of hacked code and hammer it into a dozen, complete with documentation and to coding standard. Earl Miles, who continues to raise the bar for developers. Alex Urevick-Ackelsberg, a friend and peer whose continued help with many interesting projects and modules has been invaluable. Suzi Arnold, a theming virtuoso on a level all her own. Andrew Morton, who gave me a crash course on SimpleTests during the media code sprint. Oleg Terenchuk, a generous person, a leader in the Drupal NYCcommunity, and an enthusiast for gaming in Drupal. Geoff Holden, whose contributions to the Drupal Media Player project have turned it from a pipe dream to nearly a reality. Angela Byron, an ambassador and bridge between the many, sometimes disparate, groups composing our community. And Károly Négyesi, Drupal incarnate.

Obviously, this book would never have seen the light of day were it not for its editors and reviewers. I want to thank Douglas Paterson, who championed the book in the first place. Lata Basantani, who probably pulled out some hair every time I was late with a chapter, but managed to sound nice about it from my end. The technical reviewers, James, Kristof, Bruno, and Ryan, who smoothed the rough edges of this book; if there's anything still lacking, it is through no fault of theirs. And all the other great editors at Packt: I only wrote the thing; you all made it presentable.

The person I need to thank most is my partner, Gwen Pfeifer, whom I love dearly. She has endured many sleepless nights as I've struggled over minutiae while writing this book, and has still managed to be endlessly supportive.

There are so many more people who deserve my gratitude, and I deeply fear I'll forget someone important, and so need to ask forgiveness in advance. In particular, there are dozens of maintainers, developers, and testers who are responsible for the excellent modules reviewed throughout this book, which would not be possible without their hard work. Thank you all.

About the Reviewers

James Walker is Lullabot's Director of Education where he oversees the company's public workshops, seminars and private Drupal trainings, combining his passion for both technology and teaching. A leader in the Drupal community, James is a founding member of the non-profit Drupal Association and the Drupal security team. As a long-time member of the Drupal community, James maintains over a dozen modules and has contributed countless patches to Drupal core. He is one of the authors of O'Reilly's upcoming book Using Drupal.

A long-time believer in Open Source and Open Standards, James has spent years co-ordinating Drupal's involvement with other communities such as Jabber/XMPP and, most recently, OpenID. An engaging speaker, James is a frequently requested presenter at many types of technical conferences. His humorous and informative lectures have been among the best-attended at DrupalCons, starting with the first—four years ago. James is known as "walkah" on drupal.org.

Kristof De Jaeger is a senior Drupal developer at Krimson with a focus primarily on module development. His first baby steps with Drupal were around 2005 and since then, he's been hooked helping out the community on IRC, writing modules, testing out patches, and spreading the word to everyone interested in web development.

Bruno De Bondt currently lives in Brussels, Belgium, where he does web and tech work for Indymedia.be (IMC Belgium). This involves Drupal site development and theming, system administration, and ocassional GNU/Linux support. He studied journalism in Ghent (Belgium) and Utrecht (The Netherlands), where he specialised in internet and international journalism.

After developing a website for a school project, he dived further into web development. Over the last few years, he built and managed websites for several NGOs and non-profits. After dabbling with several CMSs, he discovered Drupal in 2005, while looking for software to run the new Indymedia.be website.

The Indymedia.be site has been running on Drupal since autumn 2005. The switch to Drupal coincided with a choice of the Indymedia.be team to create a broadly oriented progressive citizen news website, instead of the more in-crowd activist website it had been before. Drupal has played a crucial role in this process, enabling Indymedia.be to run a solid and secure website, while at the same time allowing a high degree of flexibility. At the time of writing. the Indymedia.be tech team is hard at work on its new website, leveraging Drupal's capabilities even more — it's amazing what you learn in three years' time. A lot of the practices and tips discussed in this book are part of Indymedia.be's new site. Thanks Aaron!

Being a trained journalist, Bruno still does some writing work now and then. He co-authored 'Media-activisme/Don't hate the media, be the media', a media-activist guide (2004 — www.media-activism.be). He also did editing and reviewing work for 'Burgermedia', a reader discussing citizen media in Belgium and abroad (2008 — www.burgermedia.be).

Thanks to: The Indymedia.be team. All IMC'stas (Belgium and worldwide). Mark, Ekes and others of the Indymedia Drupal gang.

Dries Buytaert for posting his scripts on the web (and the Drupal community for making them what they are today). The Krimson guys for support and feedback (www.krimson.be). Joeri Poesen for being my personal PHP guru (www.symbiotix.be). Development Seed for inspiration, feedback and good times at several DrupalCons. The thousands & thousands carrying the torch high for free and open-source software.

```
http://indymedia.be
http://brunodbo.be
```

Ryan Shrout is the owner and editor-in-chief of PC Perspective, a PC hardware and technology review website. Before joining the hardware world Ryan was a CS student who worked primarily in web technologies PHP, MySQL, JavaScript, and more. He maintains and develops custom CMS systems for PC Perspective, among others, as a hobby and has recently adopted Drupal for future projects going forward. Ryan's background in a wide array of software and hardware allows him a unique view of the open-source community.

To my father, Victor, who set me on this path.

Table of Contents

Preface

Drupal Multimedia takes an in-depth look at one of the most common questions posed by new (and old) Drupal developers: How can I place images/video/audio into my site?

Drupal is an open-source Content Management System (CMS), used on thousands of sites from personal blogs to e-commerce sites to media powerhouses. Although Drupal can be easily installed and configured to quickly get a site up with all the best features one might expect, its modular building blocks can be used to customize that site to fit the required solution.

For anything beyond a simple listing of files uploaded with content, multimedia handling requires modules and techniques beyond what's supplied with the core of Drupal. Fortunately (or unfortunately, depending on your perspective), there are hundreds of modules that have been contributed by and for the community, which can handle nearly any current need. Drupal Multimedia will help you make sense of it all.

What This Book Covers

Chapter 1: It offers an in-depth introduction to Drupal and the basic modules required for most of the book. By the end of the chapter, you will have learned about the building blocks of Drupal, including nodes, users, themes, regions, and blocks. You will also have explored the Content Construction Kit (CCK) and Views, learning to use them to create custom content and display it just the way you want.

Chapter 2: It will explore the Image module, and others that depend on its functionality, to easily create image galleries and attach images to content, or even place them inline using a WYSIWYG editor.

Chapter 3: It taps the power of CCK and Views, using ImageField and ImageCache to create powerful, custom solutions for image needs. Using these modules, you'll be able to quickly create your own custom content types and display images that can be altered on the fly, for resizing, cropping, and other manipulations. You'll also learn to create slide shows, and use Embedded Media Field to pull image content from Flickr and other third-party providers.

Chapter 4: Once you learned various ways to display an image, you'll learn how to override the display, to add effects such as drop shadows and rollovers. You'll use Firebug and the Theme Developer module to investigate a theme at its most basic building blocks, jump into PHPTemplate to transform our content, and study style sheets as a mean of controlling output from a user's browser.

Chapter 5: You'll learn how to embed and display third-party video within your content, using Embedded Media Field to automatically parse and display video from an editor's pasted URL from YouTube, Blip.TV, or other providers.

Chapter 6: It will show you how to supply video from your own server. Using the techniques and modules introduced here, specifically FileField and jQuery Media, you'll learn how to create your own YouTube clone. You'll also see how to create video thumbnail links and logo overlays for rudimentary branding.

Chapter 7: It will give a brief segue into file asset management, where you will learn various methods of controlling the workflow of media in your site. You'll see how to use Node Reference to tie disparate pieces of content together. You'll also examine the Asset module as an intuitive User Interface for editors to manage media, and Media Mover as a powerful back-end solution to bring videos, images, and audio into your file system, using FTP or even email as an alternative to a browser upload for attaching media to your content. You'll also briefly examine the benefits of using a third-party solution such as Kaltura for asset management and control.

Chapter 8: You'll learn how to use the Audio module as a powerful solution for integrating audio into your site. Using the node type created by the module, you'll be able to easily and quickly embed music and podcasts into your content.

Chapter 9: Using the FileField + jQuery Media solution examined earlier, you'll see how to use that for finite and flexible control over audio content. This separates audio functionality from the node, placing it into the field, so you will have the full benefits of CCK and Views for controlling our data. you'll also examine how the Embedded Media Field can be used to embed third-party audio content with the same ease as with images and video.

Chapter 10: It explores some advanced techniques to control our audio content, creating play lists, both automatic editor-controlled and custom end-user defined. You'll also see how to allow end users to embed audio content from our sites in their own blogs, with a method that can be extrapolated for the other types of media.

In the final chapter, you'll take a look at the future of multimedia and Drupal. For the near term, you'll examine some great things coming for Drupal 7, such as Fields and better media handling in the core. You'll also take a longer view, of the role of multimedia in the semantic web, mobile media, and even experimental new types of embeddable media.

Who Is This Book For?

Drupal Multimedia is written for people interested in learning how to better control and display media on their sites. The book is written for beginners and intermediate developers, although some of the techniques are admittedly advanced. The author assumes you already have a Drupal installation to work with, but will guide you through the administration and development of your site as it applies to each section of the book. If you do not yet know how to install Drupal on a web host's server, you are directed to Drupal.org for more information. A video cast is available at `http://drupal.org/videocasts/installing-6` that can guide you through the steps of installation.

Please visit this book's companion site at DrupalMultimedia.org, where you can see live demonstrations of all the techniques explored here.

Conventions

In this book, you will find a number of styles of text that distinguish between different kinds of information. Here are some examples of these styles, and an explanation of their meaning.

Code words in text are shown as follows: "We can include other contexts through the use of the `include` directive."

A block of code will be set as follows:

```
regions[left]    = Left sidebar
regions[right]   = Right sidebar
regions[upper]   = Upper
regions[content] = Content
regions[header]  = Header
```

New terms and **important words** are introduced in a bold-type font. Words that you see on the screen, in menus or dialog boxes for example, appear in our text like this: "clicking the **Next** button moves you to the next screen".

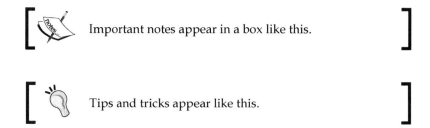

Important notes appear in a box like this.

Tips and tricks appear like this.

Reader Feedback

Feedback from our readers is always welcome. Let us know what you think about this book, what you liked or may have disliked. Reader feedback is important for us to develop titles that you really get the most out of.

To send us general feedback, simply drop an email to `feedback@packtpub.com`, making sure to mention the book title in the subject of your message.

If there is a book that you need and would like to see us publish, please send us a note in the **SUGGEST A TITLE** form on `www.packtpub.com` or email `suggest@packtpub.com`.

If there is a topic that you have expertise in and you are interested in either writing or contributing to a book, see our author guide on `www.packtpub.com/authors`.

Customer Support

Now that you are the proud owner of a Packt book, we have a number of things to help you to get the most from your purchase.

Downloading the Example Code for the Book

Visit `http://www.packtpub.com/files/code/4602_Code.zip` to directly download the example code.

The downloadable files contain instructions on how to use them.

Errata

Although we have taken every care to ensure the accuracy of our contents, mistakes do happen. If you find a mistake in one of our books—maybe a mistake in text or code—we would be grateful if you would report this to us. By doing this you can save other readers from frustration, and help us to improve subsequent versions of this book. If you find any errata, report them by visiting http://www.packtpub.com/support, selecting your book, clicking on the **let us know** link, and entering the details of your errata. Once your errata are verified, your submission will be accepted and the errata added to the list of existing errata. The existing errata can be viewed by selecting your title from http://www.packtpub.com/support.

Piracy

Piracy of copyright material on the Internet is an ongoing problem across all media. At Packt, we take the protection of our copyright and licenses very seriously. If you come across any illegal copies of our works in any form on the Internet, please provide the location address or website name immediately so we can pursue a remedy.

Please contact us at copyright@packtpub.com with a link to the suspected pirated material.

We appreciate your help in protecting our authors, and our ability to bring you valuable content.

Questions

You can contact us at questions@packtpub.com if you are having a problem with some aspect of the book, and we will do our best to address it.

Introduction and Overview

1

Drupal is an open-source **Content Management System (CMS)**, which can be used to create powerful, flexible websites that are easily configured and edited by the end users, who don't even need to know how to use HTML to harness its power. Using contributed modules to provide specialized functionality, you can use Drupal to create nearly any site that can be envisioned. Being scalable, it can be used to power anything from a community portal to a corporate network.

Drupal is the framework of choice for tens of thousands of developers and companies that build their sites based on Drupal. Drupal has been consistently rated among the top CMSs for several years.

Released as an open-source project in 2001 by its original creator, Dries Buytaert (`http://buytaert.net/`), it quickly attracted a strong community of developers and programmers. By now it is a mature and stable product that continues to evolve. With the release of Drupal 6 earlier this year, it remains a cutting-edge choice for website development.

Drupal is a database-driven dynamic web application built on PHP. As PHP is offered by most web hosts, as are MySQL and PostgreSQL, the database management systems supported by Drupal can be deployed from most server environments.

 PHP is a reflective programming language, which means that a Drupal script can observe and modify itself at runtime, allowing advanced features such as custom dynamic blocks and its template theming system.

Also, Drupal encapsulates the database in an abstract layer so that the contributed modules may access data stored on the server without knowing the implementation procedure. This allows a site to be deployed from any of the wide array of servers, using MySQL or PostgreSQL, Apache or IIS, Linux or Windows, and many other options.

Drupal has sometimes been criticized as not following **Object-Oriented Programming (OOP)**, largely because it doesn't make much use of PHP's object classes, which is far from true. In reality, Drupal standards implement OOP in an advanced and efficient way (see http://api. drupal.org/api/file/developer/topics/oop.html/6 for more discussion on this topic). Additionally, PHP 5 offers better OOP support and as Drupal moves to the requirement of this version of PHP, module maintainers will take more advantage of it.

The end result is that a site built with Drupal can be expanded and enhanced, using plug-in contributed modules and custom themes to create a powerful and unique site. It is specifically these two facets (contributed modules and custom theming) that will be explored in detail throughout this book, obviously with an eye towards multimedia.

Because of the limited space and the availability of excellent resources, this book assumes you have some basic experience of using Drupal, and that you already know how to install it on a server. In fact, to get the most out of this book, you probably want to have a test installation to test some of the techniques and ideas presented here. Besides visiting Drupal.org, you can also find more help in the Resources Appendix of this book.

Drupal's Multimedia

The Internet has literally exploded with multimedia over the past few years. We will specifically study images, audio, and video in this book, with some additional discussion of interactive media such as FLASH.

Drupal is well-suited to handling multimedia with its modular structure. However, at first glance on installation, this may not seem to be true. This is by design. The core of Drupal is meant to be fast, light, and scalable. It needs functionalities such as asset management and multimedia display that are provided by contributed modules, which must be added onto its core by developers and administrators. Finally, theme developers (or **Themers**, as these people are commonly referred to in the world of Drupal) take the resultant display and change it to meet the specifications for the site, matching content to compositions.

Due to the dichotomy between the light feel of Drupal core and the overwhelming dread of scouring through hundreds of contributed modules, the need has arisen for a book such as this, which will demonstrate how best to create a site that harnesses the power available for multimedia handling. But firstly, we need to understand the basics offered by the **Drupal core** and a few essential modules.

Drupal's Building Blocks

There are many essential components of Drupal. The basic components that we'll cover in this chapter are **Nodes** (content), **Regions** (areas of a page), **Blocks** (information placed in a specific region), **Themes** (describing how content is displayed), and **Modules** (adding new capabilities to a site). There are other essential components such as **Users** (providing individual accounts on a site), **Filters** (to filter user-generated content such as removing unwanted markup), and **Comments** (added to nodes by multiple users), but they are out of scope for this discussion (though may be touched upon in relevant sections throughout the book).

Nodes

Most content in Drupal is stored in the form of nodes. In general, if you are new to the concept, you can begin by thinking of a node as what would normally be thought of as a **blog**, **post**, or **article** in more static sites. The reality is that nodes can be far more complex yet flexible than this and may be extended in novel ways, as we'll explore throughout this book:

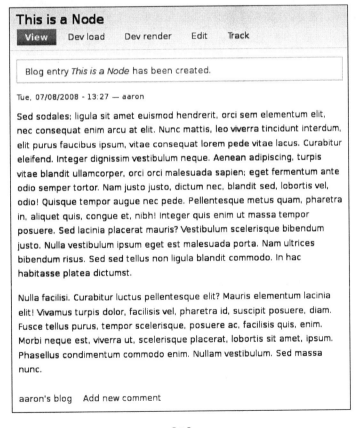

All nodes have an associated node type. This can be defined by a module such as the built-in page and blog types, contributed image, or video node types. In addition, using **Content Construction Kit** (**CCK**), you may define your own custom types and store specific information based on the needs of your site. We will explore this soon.

The basic node will have a title and a body. In general, the body will store the text, although it can be used to display multimedia in line with the text. Modules may allow other types of data known as fields, which may display a set type of multimedia in a specific place in the content, for instance. In addition, some modules such as Image attach may allow multimedia or other data to be attached to any node type.

Nodes are usually displayed in one of these three ways: as teasers, as full pages, and in views. There may be other ways of displaying node content, especially when writing custom code, but we will explore these options, which should suffice in most of the cases.

Teasers are generally smaller or shorter versions of the full content. For instance, a teaser might display the first paragraph or two with a thumbnail. On a basic default Drupal installation, once you have created some nodes, you will see an example of teasers on the front page of the site. By theming, developers may alter how a teaser is displayed.

All nodes may be viewed in full at their respective node pages, usually accessed by clicking on the title of a teaser. By default, this will display all the data stored in a node, although that may be overridden or altered in any of several ways.

The URL for the default node page view will always be at /node/[nid], replacing [nid] with the node's unique identification number. This URL may be overridden manually or with other modules such as by using the **URL path settings** section of the node submission page or automatically using the **Pathauto** module. But it will still always be accessible using /node/[nid], for example at http://www.example.com/node/225 or http://www.example.com/?q=node/225 (if not using clean URLs).

Throughout this book, when displaying a URL, we'll assume you have enabled clean URLs on your site. If you have not, you would need to prepend ?q= to a URL. For example, /admin/build/modules would be ?q=admin/build/modules. In both cases, that would be local to your site such as http://www.example.com/admin/build/modules or http://www.example.com/?q=admin/build/modules.
To enable clean URLs on your site, browse to **Administer | Site configuration | Clean URLs** at /admin/settings/clean-urls or ?q=admin/settings/clean-urls.

The **Views** module (touched upon later in this chapter) opens up many new ways of displaying information from nodes. Views may display nodes as teasers, full views, or slide shows, or may take specific parts of the data and display them in a list or a table. There are many other ways a view can display content and we will explore the more common methods in this book.

Regions and Blocks

A page is divided into several regions, each of which can be used to display content using blocks. By default, the main content of a page is displayed in the **content** region. For instance, the node content when displaying a node's page or the listing of recently published and promoted nodes on the front page. The left sidebar on a default Drupal installation is another region, as are the header, footer, and right sidebar.

> Custom regions are easily added to a theme by modifying that theme's
> `.info` file. For instance, you might specify `regions[content_top]`
> `= content top` to create that new region. Note that this is different
> than in Drupal 5, where new regions were defined in a now deprecated
> `mytheme_regions` function. We'll explore theming in more detail
> throughout the book.

You may determine what content will be displayed in what regions on the **Blocks administration** page by browsing to **Administer | Site Building | Blocks** (at `/admin/build/block`). Active blocks are shown here grouped by region, with the remainder shown in the **Disabled** section of the page.

After setting a block into a region, you can further determine its placement in the region by dragging and dropping it. Finally, by clicking on the **configure** link next to a block, you may change block-specific settings such as controlling what pages a block will be displayed on, or changing the block's title:

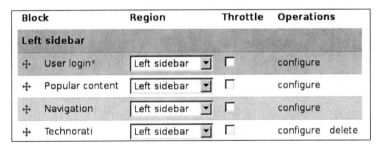

Block	Region	Throttle	Operations
Left sidebar			
✛ User login*	Left sidebar ▾	☐	configure
✛ Popular content	Left sidebar ▾	☐	configure
✛ Navigation	Left sidebar ▾	☐	configure
✛ Technorati	Left sidebar ▾	☐	configure delete

Drupal and installed modules will define many useful blocks of information such as a listing of users who are currently online (**Who's Online**), or the main **Navigation** menu. You may create custom blocks (using the **Add block** tab on the **Blocks** administration page) where you can add static text or even a short PHP script (assuming you've enabled the **PHP filter** module) for something dynamic. Using the **Views** module, you may also create blocks listing nodes that are filtered and sorted by your own criteria.

Themes

Most developers will want to format the content of their site in a manner that is different from what comes out-of-the-box. We will cover some of these methods in detail throughout the book. This is referred to as "theming", and many Drupal developers specialize as themers.

As an administrator, you may have noticed the theme section of the site. At **Administer | Site building | Themes** (at /admin/build/themes), you will see several themes that are available. These may be themes that are included with Drupal, contributed themes available from Drupal.org or other sources, and/or custom themes created specifically for the site:

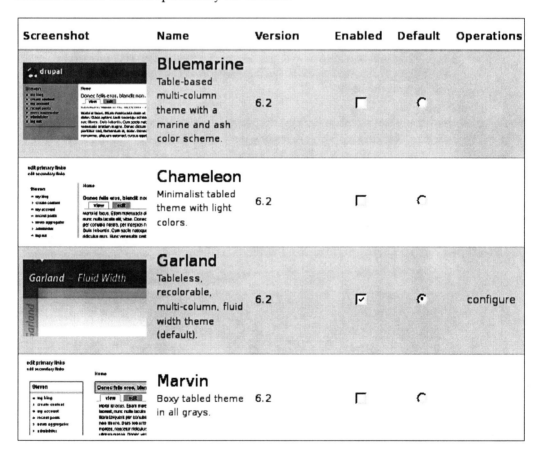

Screenshot	Name	Version	Enabled	Default	Operations
	Bluemarine Table-based multi-column theme with a marine and ash color scheme.	6.2	☐	○	
	Chameleon Minimalist tabled theme with light colors.	6.2	☐	○	
	Garland Tableless, recolorable, multi-column, fluid width theme (default).	6.2	☑	◉	configure
	Marvin Boxy tabled theme in all grays.	6.2	☐	○	

It is this third possibility of custom themes that will be of most interest to us during the course of this book. So we will need to know the basics of overriding a theme. If you are interested in learning the theming techniques that will be covered, you should probably have a custom theme to play with. For most of the examples in this book, we'll modify a copy of the **Garland** theme that comes shipped with Drupal and is enabled by default.

Contributed Modules

We will make much use of the various contributed modules throughout this book. Some of these modules, such as **Image** and **Embedded Media Field**, are specialized enough to be covered in their relevant sections. Others, such as the **Content** and **Views** modules, are essential throughout several sections. We will examine them in this chapter and explore them in more detail as needed later.

One of the strengths of Drupal is its expandability using contributed modules, and no single book could fully cover more than what many might consider the most essential, let alone the hundreds of currently available modules. This is especially so because new modules are constantly being added and old modules updated.

The modules presented in this book have been selected based on their relevance to the required tasks, their code stability, and high level of support and maintenance. All of these modules are used in production to power sites that may be small or large, and have sometimes dozens or hundreds of volunteers actively troubleshooting and maintaining them.

As you continue to explore the world of Drupal, make certain to continuously examine the available contributed modules. You can find nearly all of them at http://drupal.org/project. You can further find ongoing discussions of the development and use of the modules at http://groups.drupal.org/ in various discussion groups.

 You may also be interested in visiting the third-party site **Drupal Modules** at http://drupalmodules.com. This site allows user reviews and ratings, allowing you to read feedback about a module before choosing to install it. Such a metric, though not failsafe, can be useful when considering the hundreds of currently available modules.

Content Construction Kit (CCK)

The CCK module is a valuable contributed module that can be found on a large majority of Drupal sites. In fact, parts of it are increasingly becoming integrated into Drupal core because of its power and versatility.

As discussed earlier, content is largely defined on a site by content types for nodes. For instance, modules may be activated to provide blog, page, or video-type nodes. Using CCK, you can also define custom types for a specific purpose.

As an example you might define an article content-type, which in addition to the title and body fields automatically provided, might include a byline field, a teaser Image, and an issue reference.

As with all contributed modules, you will first need to download and install the module before using it on your site. The **CCK** module is available at `http://drupal.org/project/cck`. Once downloaded, you will need to place the entire extracted folder in the `/sites/all/modules` directory. After this, you will see the module along with all other available modules for a site by browsing to **Administer | Site Building | Modules** (at `/admin/build/modules`).

Enable that module and any other desired modules included in the **CCK** package of that screen such as **Text, Number**, or **Node Reference**. (In Drupal 5, that section is named **Content**.)

Enabled	Name	Version	Description
▽ CCK			
☑	Content	6.x-2.0-rc2	Allows administrators to define new content types. Required by: Content Copy (disabled), Content Permissions (disabled), Fieldgroup (enabled), Node Reference (enabled), Number (enabled), Option Widgets (enabled), Text (enabled), User Reference (disabled)
☐	Content Copy	6.x-2.0-rc2	Enables ability to import/export field definitions. Depends on: Content (enabled)
☐	Content Permissions	6.x-2.0-rc2	Set field-level permissions for CCK fields. Depends on: Content (enabled)
☑	Fieldgroup	6.x-2.0-rc2	Create field groups for CCK fields. Depends on: Content (enabled)
☑	Node Reference	6.x-2.0-rc2	Defines a field type for referencing one node from another. Depends on: Content (enabled), Text (enabled), Option Widgets (enabled)
☑	Number	6.x-2.0-rc2	Defines numeric field types. Depends on: Content (enabled)
☑	Option Widgets	6.x-2.0-rc2	Defines selection, check box and radio button widgets for text and numeric fields. Depends on: Content (enabled) Required by: Node Reference (enabled), User Reference (disabled)
☑	Text	6.x-2.0-rc2	Defines simple text field types. Depends on: Content (enabled) Required by: Node Reference (enabled), User Reference (disabled)
☐	User Reference	6.x-2.0-rc2	Defines a field type for referencing a user from a node. Depends on: Content (enabled), Text (enabled), Option Widgets (enabled)

Custom Content Types

Now you will be able to create your own custom content types. Continuing with the example of an Article type, you would browse to **Administer | Content management | Content types | Add content type** (at /admin/content/types/add) and fill in the appropriate fields on that page. After submitting, you would have a new content type with a title and an optional body:

Content types   List   **Add content type**   Fields

To create a new content type, enter the human-readable name, the machine-readable name, and all other relevant fields that are on this page. Once created, users of your site will be able to create posts that are instances of this content type.

Identification

Name: *

Article

The human-readable name of this content type. This text will be displayed as part of the list on the *create content* page. It is recommended that this name begin with a capital letter and contain only letters, numbers, and **spaces**. This name must be unique.

Type: *

article

The machine-readable name of this content type. This text will be used for constructing the URL of the *create content* page for this content type. This name must contain only lowercase letters, numbers, and underscores. Underscores will be converted into hyphens when constructing the URL of the *create content* page. This name must be unique.

Description:

An article is the name of our new, custom content type. In this fictitious example, we might ultimately place articles prominently on our front page, with a slide show of associated videos in the right sidebar. But that's for later chapters...

A brief description of this content type. This text will be displayed as part of the list on the *create content* page.

▷ Submission form settings

▷ Workflow settings

▷ Comment settings

Save content type

Fields

The strength of CCK is that it allows custom fields to be defined and added to the content types. Fields allow you to add any additional information to a type such as subtitles, images, and videos. Some basic fields, such as text and numbers, are included with the module. But others, such as images and files, require additional contributed modules.

To add fields, you will need to click on the **add field** link next to the new type on the resulting page from our ongoing example:

Content types	List	Add content type	Fields

Below is a list of all the content types on your site. All posts that exist on your site are instances of one of these content types.

Name	Type	Description	Operations			
Article	article	An article is the name of our new, custom content type. In this fictitious example, we might ultimately place articles prominently on our front page, with a slide show of associated videos in the right sidebar. But that's for later chapters...	edit	add field	manage fields	delete
Page	page	A *page*, similar in form to a *story*, is a simple method for creating and displaying information that rarely changes, such as an "About us" section of a website. By default, a *page* entry does not allow visitor comments and is not featured on the site's initial home page.	edit	add field	manage fields	delete
Story	story	A *story*, similar in form to a *page*, is ideal for creating and displaying content that informs or engages website visitors. Press releases, site announcements, and informal blog-like entries may all be created with a *story* entry. By default, a *story* entry is automatically featured on the site's initial home page, and provides the ability to post comments.	edit	add field	manage fields	delete

» Add a new content type

In this example, that would bring you to `/admin/content/node-type/article/` `add_field`). You'll name the field, select the type of field such as text or image, and submit the page to see the configuration page for the field. Here you can further define things such as setting a maximum image resolution or allowed values. In this example, we'll create a text field named Subtitle:

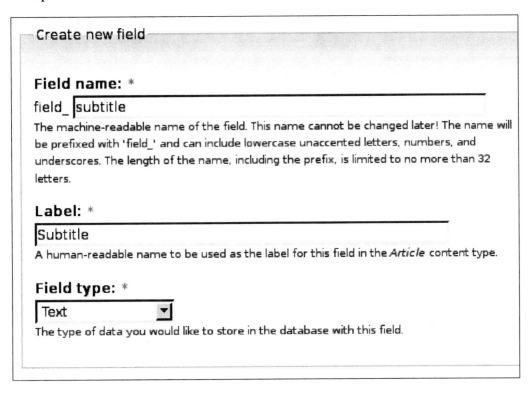

The resulting page contains sections that will affect the specific field. Additionally, because created fields can be shared among content types, you can further define settings that will affect all similarly shared fields.

Home › Administer › Content management › Article

Subtitle

Edit   **Manage fields**   Display fields   Add field   Add group

Created field *Subtitle*.

Article basic information

Label:

Subtitle

Widget type:

Text field ▾

Change basic information

Article settings

These settings apply only to the *Subtitle* field as it appears in the *Article* content type.

▷   Default value

Display in group:

<none> ▾

Select a group, in which the field will be displayed on the editing form.

Help text:

Instructions to present to the user below this field on the editing form.
Allowed HTML tags: <a> <b> <big> <code> <del> <em> <i> <ins> <pre> <q> <small> <span> <strong> <sub> <sup> <tt> <ol> <ul> <li> <p>

Global settings

These settings apply to the *Subtitle* field in every content type in which it appears.

☐ Required

Number of values:

1   ▾

Select a specific number of values for this field, or 'Unlimited' to provide an 'Add more' button so the users can add as many values as they like.
Warning! Changing this setting after data has been created could result in the loss of data!

Text processing:

○ Plain text

⦿ Filtered text (user selects input format)

Maximum length:

The maximum length of the field in characters. Leave blank for an unlimited size.

▷   Allowed values

Save field settings

Once a field has been created, you may change the order of its display by dragging the icon to the left of the field on the resulting page, which you can also find by browsing to **Administer | Content management | Article | Manage fields** (at `admin/content/node-type/article/fields`):

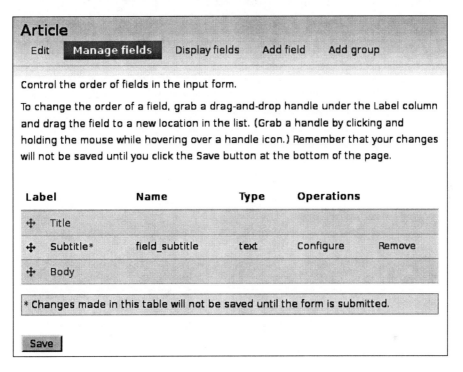

User Permissions

We can define permissions for our users, who can be grouped by roles. For instance, we might have an edit role, whose users are able to create article content. First, we'll define a new role by going to **Administer | User management | Roles** (at `/admin/user/roles`):

Roles

Roles allow you to fine tune the security and administration of Drupal. A role defines a group of users that have certain privileges as defined in user permissions. Examples of roles include: anonymous user, authenticated user, moderator, administrator and so on. In this area you will define the *role names* of the various roles. To delete a role choose "edit".

By default, Drupal comes with two user roles:

○ Anonymous user: this role is used for users that don't have a user account or that are not authenticated.

○ Authenticated user: this role is automatically granted to all logged in users.

Name	Operations	
anonymous user	locked	edit permissions
authenticated user	locked	edit permissions
editor	edit role	edit permissions
	Add role	

You would then visit the **User Permissions** settings browsing to **Administer | User management | Permissions** (at `/admin/user/permissions`), where you can set permissions for various roles such as allowing editors to **create article content**. You will see the permissions for all content types under the **node module** section of the form.

In Drupal 5, the **Permissions** page was known as **Access Control**, and could be found by browsing to **Administer | User management | Access control** (at `/admin/user/access`).

Permission	anonymous user	authenticated user	editor
node module			
access content	☑	☑	☐
administer content types	☐	☐	☐
administer nodes	☐	☐	☐
create article content	☐	☐	☑
create page content	☐	☐	☐
create story content	☐	☐	☐
delete any article content	☐	☐	☑
delete any page content	☐	☐	☐
delete any story content	☐	☐	☐
delete own article content	☐	☐	☐
delete own page content	☐	☐	☐
delete own story content	☐	☐	☐
delete revisions	☐	☐	☐
edit any article content	☐	☐	☑
edit any page content	☐	☐	☐
edit any story content	☐	☐	☐
edit own article content	☐	☐	☑
edit own page content	☐	☐	☐
edit own story content	☐	☐	☐
revert revisions	☐	☐	☑
view revisions	☐	☐	☑

To give a user the new role, we would then need to edit his or her user account. We can find a list of recent users at **Administer | User management | Users** (at `admin/user/user`), where we can edit them:

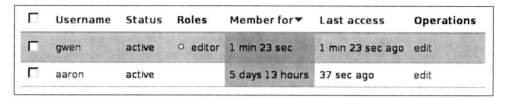

	Username	Status	Roles	Member for ▼	Last access	Operations
☐	gwen	active	○ editor	1 min 23 sec	1 min 23 sec ago	edit
☐	aaron	active		5 days 13 hours	37 sec ago	edit

Creating Content

Once you have created a new content type and set its permissions, you may create new content of that type by browsing to **Create content** and clicking on the new type (in this case at `/node/add/article`):

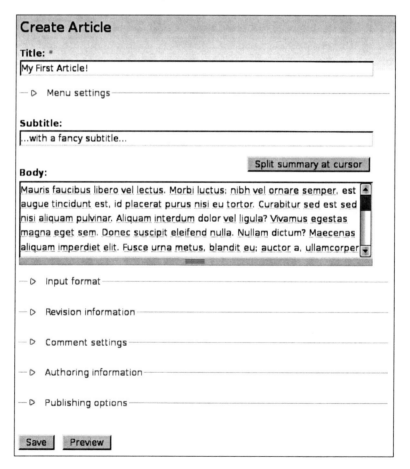

Views

Views is another contributed module that is found on many Drupal sites. It is used to create custom listings of nodes that are filtered and sorted using unique criteria, and displayed in pages and/or blocks as needed.

These views may be replicated in other ways such as by using custom SQL queries. But most developers and administrators will probably find the administration forms used to build a view much easier to manage, particularly for complex arrangements.

A view can take data from many sources such as specific fields of nodes or user information, filter them for desired criteria, and sort them in nearly any order. The **Views** and other contributed modules expose several default views that may be activated and overridden on a site. For instance, you might override the default front page view to display only promoted nodes of an article content type.

 If you are familiar with **Views** from Drupal 5, you will be pleasantly surprised by **Views 2** for Drupal 6. The engine has been rewritten from the ground up, allowing for new features such as creating views from data other than nodes. Additionally, the User Interface (UI) has been completely revamped using AJAX. This means the information you need when administering a view is all in one place, with a system of tabs and drawers to sort and access it, rather than the older system of collapsible field sets. If you are building a view for Drupal 5, the steps outlined here are largely the same, but the UI is considerably different.

View Administration

As with the **Content** module (and all other contributed modules), you will need to first upload the module directory into the /sites/all/modules folder. The **Views** module is available at http://drupal.org/project/views. Once present, you will activate it at **Administer | Site building | Modules** (at /admin/build/modules). On that page, you'll note that several other related modules are also available in the **Views** package. For the examples in this book, you will need at a minimum to activate **Views** and **Views UI**.

When you browse to **Administer | Site building | Administer views** (at `/admin/build/views`), you will see the system default views interspersed with any custom views you've created:

Default Node view: **archive** (default)	Enable
Path: archive *Block, Page*	Display a list of months that link to content for that month.
Normal Node view: **articles_popular** (articles)	Edit | Export | Clone | Delete
Path: articles/popular *Block, Page*	Displays a listing of the site's most Popular Articles.
Default Node view: **backlinks** (default)	Enable
Path: node/%/backlinks *Block, Page*	Displays a list of nodes that link to the node, using the search backlinks table.
Default Comment view: **comments_recent** (default)	Enable
Title: Recent comments Path: comments/recent *Block, Page*	Contains a block and a page to list recent comments; the block will automatically link to the page, which displays the comment body as well as a link to the node.
Default Node view: **frontpage** (default)	Edit | Export | Clone | Disable
Path: frontpage *Feed, Page*	Emulates the default Drupal front page; you may set the default home page path to this view to make it your front page.

 If you have a lot of views on your site, you may control the order on this page with the drop-down selection filters at the top of the screen. Additionally, you may enter an optional **View** tag when initializing the view, which will allow you to sort them by functionality on the administrative screen.

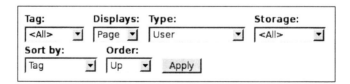

Creating a New View

You can easily create a new view from scratch by clicking on the **Add** tab, which brings you to /admin/build/views/add. However, for this example, we're going to clone an existing view so that we can see how they're set up while building it.

Click on the **Enable** link to the far right of the **frontpage** view. This enables the view on your site. Then click on the **Clone** link associated with that view, which will show you how the front page is created by default. You will be brought to the **Clone view frontpage** page (at /admin/build/views/clone/frontpage):

Clone view frontpage

View name: *

frontpage

This is the unique name of the view. It must contain only alphanumeric characters and underscores; it is used to identify the view internally and to generate unique theming template names for this view. If overriding a module provided view, the name must not be changed or instead a new view will be created.

View description:

Emulates the default Drupal front page; you may set the def

This description will appear on the Views administrative UI to tell you what the view is about.

View tag:

default   O

Enter an optional tag for this view; it is used only to help sort views on the administrative page.

View type:

⦿ Node
Nodes are a Drupal site's primary content.

○ Comment
Comments are responses to node content.

○ File
Files maintained by Drupal and various modules.

○ Node revision
Node revisions are a history of changes to nodes.

○ Term
Taxonomy terms are attached to nodes.

○ User
Users who have created accounts on your site.

○ Access log
Stores site access information.

○ Twitter message
Stores Twitter status messages.

The view type is the primary table for which information is being retrieved. The view type controls what arguments, fields, sort criteria and filters are available, so once this is set it **cannot be changed**.

Next

On the resultant screen, you'll be able to change the name and description of your new view and the tag, if desired. Although you can't change the type when cloning a view, when creating a view from scratch, you'll be able to select one of many **View types** such as **Node**, **Comment**, or **User**. This means you can create a view that is a listing of users just as easily as a listing of nodes or comments.

Change the name to `articles_recent` and describe the view appropriately. If you like, you can change the **View tag** to `articles`, to make sorting views easier in the future. Then click **Next**:

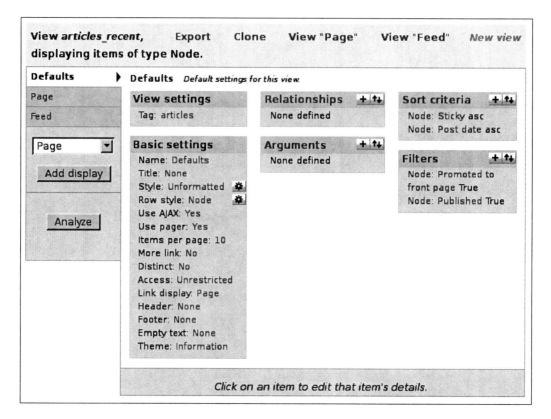

Basic Settings

On the left of the configuration screen, you'll see drawers for **Defaults**, **Page**, **Feed**, and some form elements to add new displays and analyze our view. By clicking on each drawer in turn you'll be able to see the different displays for our view, each of which can override the defaults to format a view in a specific way.

The **Basic settings** section controls things such as the **Title** displayed for the view, the **Style** to display the data, for example, a **List** or **Table**, the number of **Items per page**, who can **Access** a particular view, and similar items. We'll leave these alone for now.

Using the **Filters** section on the right, we can specify which nodes will be returned for our view. In this particular case, we want to filter nodes by their type, as we only want to display the **Article** nodes we created earlier:

Press the "+" button next to **Filters** to add a new filter. This will show all available filters. We can select **Node** from the **Groups** selector to make it easier to find the **Node: Type** box, which we will select before pressing **Add**.

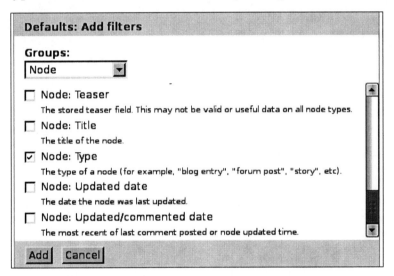

The section will be replaced with further options to specify how to filter the view. We will select our **Article** type and press **Update** here:

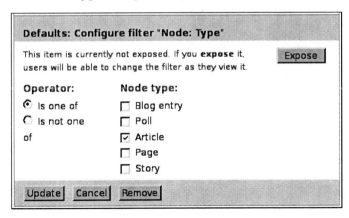

Next, click on the link for **Node: Promoted to front page** and then press the **Remove** button, as we want this view to retrieve all articles, regardless of whether they have been promoted.

 If you expose a filter, then it will also show up under **Exposed Filters**, where you may set further options. Exposed filters will be displayed at the top of a view, allowing the user to set those options to determine which nodes to display.

Finally, change the title (in the **Basic settings**) to **Articles** by clicking on **None**, entering the new title in the new text field below, and pressing **Update**.

Page Views

Now we'll set up the page. Click on the **Page** drawer to the left, just below **Defaults**. This section will determine how the view is selected and displayed as a page, in this case from /frontpage, as seen in the **Page settings** section:

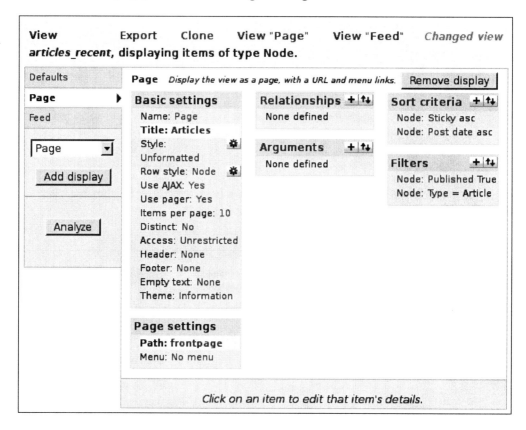

Click on **frontpage** next to **Path** within **Page settings**, and change the path to **articles**. After you press **Update**, do the same for the feed by visiting the **Feed** drawer and changing the path from `rss.xml` to `articles/rss.xml`:

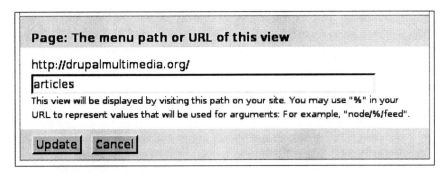

Then you can select **Block** from the selector above **Add display**, and press that button. This will create a new display for the view similar to **Page** and **Feed**. The only changes we need to make there are to set it to four items per page, rather than the default of 10, add a **More** link (which will allow users to click through to the page when there are more than four items), and to turn off the pager.

When doing each of these, we'll need to override the default values by clicking on the **Override** button that will appear in the information area (which will add the message **Status: using overridden values** above that area).

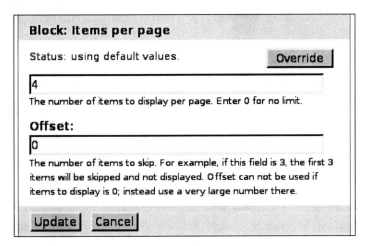

You may then **Save** the view, so we can see the results.

Advanced Views Options

The **Arguments** fieldset is used to create some flexibility from the URL. Thus, by setting the arguments here, you might have a gallery of all recently posted videos with a URL of `/videos`, and further display of only videos in a certain vocabulary with `/videos/[vocabulary-id]`, and finally only videos in a certain taxonomy term with `/videos/[vocabulary-id]/[term-id]`. Note that if there are **Arguments** set for the view, then those will be combined with **Filters** when selecting the nodes to display.

> The **Sort criteria** will determine the order to display the selected nodes for the view. The **frontpage** and **article** views will first display nodes marked as **sticky**, and then set them in reverse order of creation time. We could easily change the order, for instance by sorting articles by popularity, author, or time of most recent comments.

Advanced Theming

Because overriding the display of default content is essential in creating a professional site, we'll explore a few techniques that any serious developer or themer should keep in a toolkit. Template files are used to separate PHP code from the HTML, which is more familiar to many themers and designers. Sometimes we need to create custom regions, which also we will explore. And finally, we need to know how to override specific content at its most basic element, the theme function.

Adding a New Theme

It is certainly possible and sometimes preferable to start a new theme from scratch. However, for this book, we'll modify an existing theme to give ourselves a jumpstart.

From your FTP client, you'll need to make a copy of the **Garland** theme directory. You'll need to copy the entire **Garland** directory from `/themes/garland` to `/sites/all/themes`. Then rename the new **Garland** directory, for example to **mytheme**. This folder name will be used as the machine name of your new theme.

If you don't already have a themes directory in `/sites/all`, you'll need to make one first. When checking for themes, Drupal will look in the appropriate site directory such as `/sites/example.com/themes`. Then it will look in `/sites/all/themes`, and finally in the root `/themes` directory.

By placing contributed, custom, and overridden themes in the /sites directory, you can accomplish several things. First, it will override a theme in the root /themes directory. Secondly, if it is placed in /sites/all/themes, it will be made available to sites sharing the same codebase. (Conversely, it will only show up for a specific site if it isin something like /sites/example.com/themes.) Finally, it will be easier to update the site as Drupal evolves, since you will be able to simply update to a later version of Drupal without worrying about theme overrides in the root directory.

> As you may have noticed from this example, Drupal allows multiple sites to share the same codebase. In such a case, each site would need its own subdirectory within the /sites folder such as /sites/example.com for http://example.com, or /sites/mysite.com for http://mysite.com. Any further subdirectories within that folder will be made available only to that site. Additionally, multiple sites may even share the same database, assuming that they have separate database table prefixes specified in the **Advanced options** section during installation.

You will also need to change the garland.info file to mytheme.info (or whatever name you have chosen). Also, edit that file and change the line that reads name = Garland to read something like name = My Theme. (You will not have a .info file for your theme in Drupal 5, so this will not apply in that case.)

After creating your new folder and making the necessary changes, you will browse to **Administer | Site Building | Themes** (at /admin/build/themes) on your site and enable the theme. You will also make the theme the default and disable the other themes. However, you may wish to keep another theme (such as the original **Garland**) as the default theme during the development and instead set the new theme on your user account edit page.

Finally, you may wish to keep a different theme layout for administration pages, particularly if your theme will not lend itself to the wide tables sometimes seen on those pages. In that case, you will browse to the Administration theme settings page at **Administer | Site Configuration | Administration theme** (at /admin/settings/admin) and set it to something basic like **Garland**.

Once you have enabled your new theme, you'll be ready to begin development on it. This is largely achieved by writing template files, which are contained in the theme directory and end with .tpl.php in their filenames. We will cover the basics of this in the template files section of this chapter, and in more detail throughout the book.

As the **Garland** theme it is installed by default on every new Drupal installation, we have chosen to use it throughout this book. But when developing a site for production, you may wish to start from another theme or even entirely from scratch. You can see many contributed themes for Drupal at http://drupal.org/project/themes. Additionally, you can see live previews of many of those themes at The Theme Garden (at http://themegarden.org/). Finally, consider the **Zen** theme, available at http://drupal.org/project/zen, which is meant to offer a no-frills, standards-compliant base theme. You may find its excellent documentation and growing community of developers and themers to be most suitable.

Basic Template Files

By default, Drupal uses **PHPTemplate** to power its themes. This flexible and powerful engine allows themers to wrap specific content in HTML snippets contained in specific files and functions. Themers can do all their work without knowing how to program, but if they are willing to explore the world of PHP, they have all the power of that scripting language to bring to bear on their themes.

There are other engines available for Drupal, notably **Smarty theme engine**, which use **Smarty Template Engine** syntax. However, this book assumes you are using **PHPTemplate**.

At its most basic, a theme will contain a page.tpl.php file. This file will wrap all the content to be displayed in the required HTML tags to feed to the user's browser. Several PHP variables are made available for theming, which generally contain either content to be displayed or directives to tell us how to display content.

Also, a theme folder will contain one or more stylesheets such as **Garland**'s style.css, which is the basic stylesheet to be used by that theme. The theme's .info file will contain a list of stylesheets to be included on a page. We will explore **Cascading Style Sheets (CSS)**, which are necessary to control the output of our media.

Nodes are generally displayed using special template files in the themes folder. In addition to the default node.tpl.php, each node type may have its own template file, which will be used to wrap node content when provided. These are named by appending the node's machine-readable name to the filename. For instance, we might have a node-image.tpl.php file to wrap **Image** nodes, node-external_video.tpl.php for a custom **External Video** node type, and node-article.tpl.php for the **Article** content type we created earlier.

The `template.php` file contains functions made available to the theme, many of which are used to provide files to override the default theme functions offered by Drupal modules. This is an important concept that will be explained soon.

Other template files may be created in this folder to override how content is displayed. For instance, `block.tpl.php` and `comment.tpl.php` will respectively wrap blocks and comments with HTML. Any theme function available in Drupal may be overridden in this fashion, although some more obscure functions will require more of an understanding on how content is created in Drupal. Fortunately, there are tools available such as the **Theme Developer Module** (which we'll see in *Images for Themers*, chapter 4) to make this task easier.

Custom Regions

So you've created a new theme as outlined in the **Themes** section earlier. You've explored the files there, and are ready to begin overriding your theme.

One of your first tasks might be creating custom regions for blocks. Let's say you want a new block above the main content where you'll highlight articles and videos on the front page.

By default, you already have a **content** region. However, any blocks you activate in this region will be displayed below the page's main content.

This requires that you override your theme's region. To do this, you will need to edit the theme's `.info` file, in our case `mytheme.info`.

You will need to redefine all your regions, and enter your new region(s) by adding the following to the file:

```
regions[left]    = Left sidebar
regions[right]   = Right sidebar
regions[upper]   = Upper
regions[content] = Content
regions[header]  = Header
regions[footer]  = Footer
```

In order to register this change (or any change in the info file), you will need to visit **Administer | Site building | Themes** (at `/admin/build/themes`). Also note that you must enter all the desired regions when adding a new one even if the defaults are not listed originally in the file, as an override to the regions will remove the defaults entirely. For instance, if we were only to add `regions[upper] = Upper`, then only that region and the content would appear on a page with none of the other desired regions.

As themes in Drupal 5 don't have an info file, you would need to invoke the region's hook for the theme, in this case by creating a mytheme_regions function. See http://drupal.org/node/29139 for more information.

This will make any new regions available to Drupal, in our case creating an additional region labeled **upper**. The keys on the left of the array ('upper', 'right', and so on) define the variable names for the regions in your page.tpl.php file. The values on the right side Upper, Right sidebar, and so on will be the names for the regions as displayed on the Blocks administration page.

Once you have defined your regions in the template.php file, you need to also make sure that any new regions are displayed in the page.tpl.php file. You'll be able to display a region simply by printing its associated variable (as defined in the region array). For instance, our new **upper** region will be displayed by printing the $upper variable.

If you are following this example and have overridden the **Garland** theme, then next you will find the text <?php if ($breadcrumb): print $breadcrumb; endif; ?> in the file. Now add the following just below it:

```php
<?php if ($upper): ?>
  <div id="upper">
    <?php print $upper; ?>
  </div>
<?php endif; ?>
```

This will ensure that the upper region is displayed only if there is a value in that variable, which will only be true if you set blocks to display in that region. It will further enclose this region in a unique HTML div that may be customized using the CSS stylesheets.

You will be able to add blocks into this region from **Administer | Site building | Blocks** (at /admin/build/block). This new region will appear below the breadcrumb on a page, but before any help messages, titles, content, and so on:

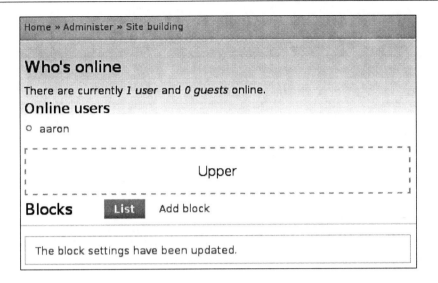

 You may notice the combination of PHP code within `<?php ?>` and HTML (such as `<div></div>`). This is one of the strengths of PHPTemplate. It allows a themer to work with the familiar markup of HTML to easily insert useful snippets of code or to print PHP variables within the markup. Within the template (`.tpl.php`) files, you need to ensure that all PHP code is contained within `<?php ?>`.

Theme Function Overrides

Any content provided by modules in Drupal may be overridden in the theme. If you know in general what theme function is creating the content, you will also know the template file or function to create.

For instance, if you want to display individual comments with **reply/edit/delete** links just below the comment's title rather than after its content, you would edit `comment.tpl.php` in `/sites/all/themes/mytheme` to move the code printing the links to just below the title line, so it reads:

```
<h3><?php print $title ?></h3>
<?php if ($links): ?>
  <div class="links"><?php print $links ?></div>
<?php endif; ?>
```

Often you may wish to override a theme that is not provided as a file in the default theme. In these cases, you will need to find the function in the code, and either create a template file (`tpl.php`) for the markup or create a theme function override in `template.php`. In some cases, especially for a short snippet of code, it may be easier to create the theme function override. If you make it available as a `tpl.php` file, this may be easier for themers to work with, particularly if they don't have much coding experience. Also, some theme functions may be more suitable in that format such as when they create a lot of markup in their output.

For the first example, let's say your editor doesn't like the **>** character in the breadcrumbs at the top of the page, and would rather display **»** between each menu item there.

This is suitable for a theme function override and, in fact, is already available in **Garland**'s `template.php`. The code for this follows after first searching the Internet to see that the HTML character code for **»** is **»**. Simply rewrite the included function as follows:

```
function phptemplate_breadcrumb($breadcrumb) {
  if (!empty($breadcrumb)) {
    return '<div class="breadcrumb">'. implode(' &raquo; ',
$breadcrumb) .'</div>';
  }
}
```

 The **»** character is officially known as a guillemet, or right angle quote. It is used to demarcate quotes in French and other languages.

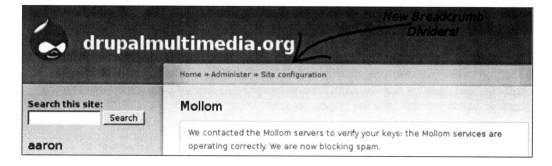

Our next request is to change the text that reads **Comment viewing options** above comments to read **Comment Controls**. (Comment viewing options are set by browsing to **Administer | Content management | Content types** – `admin/content/types` – and selecting the content type to configure. In Drupal 5, they're set globally at **Administer | Content management | Comments | Settings** – `admin/content/comments/settings`.)

Garland has no built-in override for comment controls, so we'll need to hunt through our code to find this. We know that comments are displayed using the comment module, which is found in the /modules/comment directory. So we open the comment.module file in our editor. Searching for the text **Comment viewing options**, we see the output is generated with the theme_comment_controls function.

To override a theme function, we simply rewrite our new function in template.php, replacing the theme_ in the function name with phptemplate_. So for this example, we will copy the code from the function, place it in template.php in our new theme directory, and make our changes:

```
function phptemplate_comment_controls($form) {
  $output = '<div class="container-inline">';
  $output .= drupal_render($form);
  $output .= '</div>';
  $output .= '<div class="description">'. t('Select your preferred way
    to display the comments and click "Save settings" to activate your
                                        changes.') .'</div>';
  return theme('box', t('Super-Duper Comment Controls'), $output);
}
```

Important note: When overriding theme functions, you must register new changes in the database (as of Drupal 6). To do so, you will either need to clear your cache (the easiest method being to install the Devel module from http://drupal.org/project/devel and use its provided links) or run the drupal_rebuild_theme_registry() function. While developing a theme, you may choose to add that function to the top of the template.php file, so it is run every time a page is loaded. However, if you do this, make certain to remove it before moving the site into production.

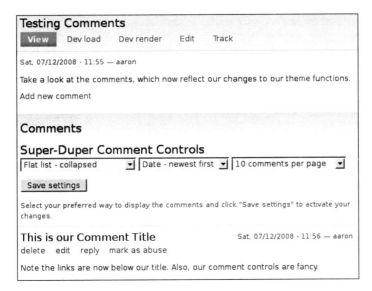

You could also have named this function something like `mytheme_comment_controls`. In fact, though the **Garland** theme doesn't follow this advice, the official policy is to do that and avoid conflicts when using sub-themes. However, there is also a strong case for using a `phptemplate_` prefix. Using the `phptemplate_` prefix makes your theme more portable. So if you later change the name of the theme or copy it to another directory for further development, you won't need to change all your `mytheme_` references to `newtheme_`.

 A useful online reference is the Drupal API found at `http://api.drupal.org`. From here, we can find definitions for all core functions, as well as topics of specific interest such as `http://api.drupal.org/api/group/themeable/6`.

Template Files Revisited

Some theme functions lend themselves well to being overridden using a template (`.tpl.php`) file. Our emboldened editor now asks us to make some overrides to the forum page, so that the link that says **Post new Forum topic** is repeated at the bottom of the screen.

All modules (as of Drupal 6) must register their themeable functions using a `hook_theme` function. This means that you can scan that function to quickly find themes that may be overridden.

Thus, we read the `forum_theme` function at `http://api.drupal.org/api/function/forum_theme/6` and see the following:

```
'forums' => array(
    'template' => 'forums',
    'arguments' => array('forums' => NULL, 'topics' => NULL,
    'parents' => NULL, 'tid' => NULL, 'sortby' => NULL,
    'forum_per_page' => NULL),
),
```

This looks promising, so we look up `theme_forums` at the Drupal API. However, it turns up nothing, so we double-check by searching for that function in the forum module. No luck!

It turns out that modules (starting with Drupal 6) may also define their own template files. Knowing this, we scan the forum module directory at `/modules/forum` and discover several template files there, including `forums.tpl.php`.

Note that if you're using Drupal 5, you would actually need to override `theme_forum_display`, which turns out to be a trickier business involving the use of the obsolete `_phptemplate_callback` in `template.php`. See `http://drupal.org/node/11811` for more information.

Finally, we copy `forums.tpl.php` to our theme directory and override it as follows, duplicating our links:

```php
<?php if ($forums_defined): ?>
<div id="forum">
  <?php print theme('links', $links); ?>
  <?php print $forums; ?>
  <?php print $topics; ?>
  <?php print theme('links', $links); ?>
</div>
<?php endif; ?>
```

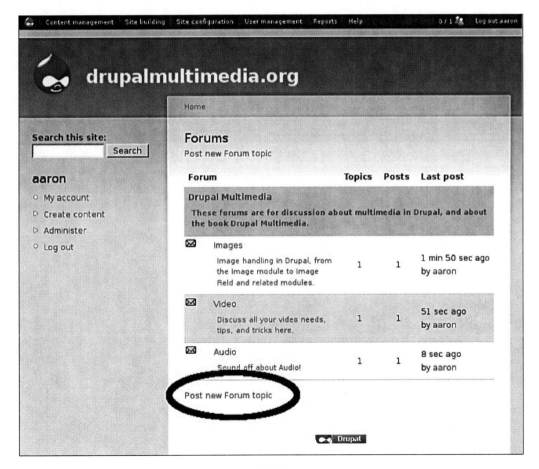

Summary

We now have enough basic knowledge to begin integrating multimedia in our Drupal sites. We have learned about Nodes, which are the basic building blocks for content. We discovered that several contributed modules, including the invaluable **CCK** and **Views** modules, may be used to create and format our content. We now know that blocks are displayed in regions, and that themes control all the output of a page. We have further learned that any theme function in Drupal may be overridden at the theme level, using either a direct override (with a `phptemplate_` or `mytheme_` function), or in many cases by creating a template file ending with `tpl.php`.

In the next chapter, we will delve into the rich world of images.

2
Images for Admins and Editors

One of the most important issues for an administrator of a site is how to display the images. Whether for a multimedia paradise with thousands of photos uploaded every day or for a largely static brochure site for a local mom and pop, the administrator needs to put some thought into how images will be uploaded and displayed.

Fortunately for us, the Web has a long history of displaying images, and hundreds of people have put countless hours in creating some fantastic tools in Drupal to help us meet our ends. This chapter will introduce us to some of the common techniques of handling images and show us how to make our jobs as administrators and editors easier.

Unfortunately, there are endless requirements for images on a site, and literally dozens of modules that have been created to handle custom needs. An entire book could easily be written on images in Drupal alone, which would leave us with no space to cover other media elements.

Thus, we'll cover enough to get you started and learn some powerful techniques that may be used in a wide array of unique circumstances.

What Does Our Site Want?

Before we install anything, we need to overview what is needed for our site. We've spent long hours banging at a module, trying to make it fit into the unique design required for a particular application. Some planning and a basic understanding of the tools available will go a long way towards coming up with a perfect solution.

For the purposes of this chapter, we will explore three basic needs: an image gallery, teaser thumbnails, and images embedded in content. Many image requirements can be generalized into these categories, and after reading this chapter you should be ready to create a basic framework for most solutions.

Creating a Gallery

Our first fictitious example is to create an image gallery for a local artists' co-operative. We have just agreed to set up a showcase site for **Seaside Treasures**, a shop that showcases and sells works created by local artists. We want to create something that looks nice, is easy for computer-illiterate artists to use, and will be quick to set up (since we're volunteering our time).

Being new to Drupal, having maybe set up a blog or two, we know there are options for image handling. But we also know that those options are not currently built into the core, and that means a visit to the contributed module repository (found at `http://drupal.org/project/Modules`). Taking a quick look, we're excited by the possibilities offered for displaying images, but overwhelmed by the sheer number of contributed modules listed (over 450 modules in the category of **Content Display** and over 150 in **Media** at the time of this writing).

What to choose? **Acidfree Albums**? **Gallery**? The aptly named **Image**? The long answer is that there are many options available and ultimately you'll need to explore them to find the best solutions to carry in your Drupal toolbox.

To get you started, however, we're going to cut through all that and show how you can use what Drupalers have used for years to get the job done.

For our first example, here is a screenshot of what we're aiming for. This is a run-of-the-mill gallery with a listing of thumbnails that, when clicked, will show a page with a larger image. Once you have your basic site configured, setting this up will take only a few minutes, leaving you with the time to work on that cool project you've been putting off:

Baskets

Painstakingly woven by a community of burned-out web developers.

There is 1 image in this gallery

Last updated: Wed, 10/24/2007 - 11:01

Paintings

These paintings are fictitiously available at our shop.

There are 2 images in this gallery

Last updated: Wed, 10/24/2007 - 11:01

Photographs

These are photographs shared in the Creative Commons.

There is 1 image in this gallery

Last updated: Wed, 10/24/2007 - 11:01

Sculpture

These are sculptures we'd like to have in our store (but don't, since it's not a real store).

Image Module

To reproduce this gallery, we're going to use the **Image** module available at `http://drupal.org/project/image`. In conjunction with this we'll also install the **Image Gallery** module, which is contributed in the same download.

After you've enabled both modules, you will have a new content type available for your site that is automatically named **Image**. You can add an image now if you'd like to, visiting **Create content | Image** (at /node/add/image) and uploading the image. You'll have a screen like the following:

Create Image

Title: *

▷   Menu settings

Image:

[   ]   **Browse...**

Click "Browse..." to select an image to upload.

Image Galleries:

- None selected - ▼

Split summary at cursor

Body:

▷   Input format

☐ Rebuild derivative images.

Check this to rebuild the derivative images for this node.

The first time you visit an image node submission page (or visit the image settings page), you'll likely get a message saying something like this: **The directory sites/example.com/files/images has been created. The directory sites/example.com/files/images/temp has been created.** The first directory will be used to store images created for image nodes and derived images. The **temp** directory will be used to temporarily store images during the upload process, and will be automatically emptied of orphaned temporary images periodically during cron sweeps. (Once configured, the cron script will run automatically every hour or so. You can find more information at http://drupal.org/cron.)

This couldn't be simpler. All you need to do is upload your images using the browse button, enter a title, and optionally write a brief description in the body text area. Preview it if you want, or just hit **submit** and you will have a new image on your site. (You won't actually see the **Image Galleries** drop-down depicted here until you've set up at least one gallery. We'll deal with that next.)

Assuming you haven't changed any defaults, your new images will also appear on the front page, although probably not formatted as well as they would be in the gallery, once we've set that up.

Gallery Categories

If you set up one or more galleries for your images, you'll discover that Drupal automatically sorts your images into categories so that you can set up sections for **Ceramics**, **Paintings**, **Bead Work**, and **Wood Carvings**.

To do this, go to **Administer | Content management | Image galleries** (at /admin/content/image). Here you will find a list of any galleries you have set up for the site, which will be empty at first. Click on the **Add gallery** tab and enter a name for your new gallery (which in our case will be **Arts & Crafts**).

After adding at least one, you may nest new image galleries below others by selecting the appropriate gallery from the parent drop-down selector. You'll also be able to control the order the galleries appear in using the **Weight** selector: Galleries with a lower number will appear before those with a higher number, and alphabetically if they share the same weight. For instance, you might have **Basket Weaving**, **Candles**, and **Dryer Lint Sculpture** as categories under the **Folk Art** gallery, which in turn is below the **Arts & Crafts**.

Now you can go back to your original image, click on the **Edit** tab, select one of your new galleries from the drop-down list, and press the **Submit** button. Then browse to **Administer | Site building | Menus** (at /admin/build/menu). Under the **Navigation** menu, you will probably see **Image galleries (disabled)**. You will need to enable this menu item for it to show up in your navigation menu by clicking **enable** at the end of that row and pressing **Submit** on the following screen.

After doing this, you will be able to see your new gallery by browsing to **Image galleries** (at **image**). You will also notice that the breadcrumb changes for your content, so it will list the gallery at the top of the page (with something like **Home | Image galleries | Arts & Crafts | Mobiles**).

When you visit the gallery page, you will also note that any description you entered for the gallery will be listed there with the thumbnail of the most recent image entered in that gallery to represent it.

The **Image Gallery** module is actually an extension of the **Taxonomy** module included in the Drupal core. Taxonomy is one of the many features that allow Drupal to stand out, giving it a way to powerfully control the flow of content through a site.

We won't delve too deeply into the wonderful world of Drupal's taxonomy with its ability to create complex and rich nested, multiple hierarchal vocabularies. It will suffice to say that you can harness the power of taxonomy and folksonomy to organize your site in a logical and useful way that makes it easy for you, your users, and even Google to find exactly what you or they are looking for in seconds.

Gallery categories, although they use the same engine as the rest of Drupal taxonomy, are generally configured and accessed from a different location in the menu tree. This is to allow the gallery to work automatically without any special configuration. Technically, the Image Gallery creates a unique taxonomy **vocabulary**, and each gallery is a term beneath it. You can see this by browsing to **Administer | Content management | Taxonomy** (at /admin/content/taxonomy). (In Drupal 5, **Taxonomy** was sometimes referred to as **Categories** such as in the menu path.)

Image Size Settings

You've probably noticed by now that your image is presented in two different sizes, both of which may be different than the original uploaded size. This happens automatically with help from the **Image** module.

You'll also see that various sizes are available when viewing an image node page: By default, you'll see a link under the image for **Thumbnail**. If you click on this, you will see the image displayed in a new size and a link to another size labeled **Preview**, which is the size an image is normally displayed in when visiting its node page.

The **Original** size is available only to users who have the **view original images** access setting, so you won't see this link unless you add that setting to a role. You can see all access settings for your site by visiting **Administer | User management | Permissions** (at /admin/user/permissions). Note that you may also wish to set up a new role for editors who might need the **create image content** access setting. User roles are created at **Administer | User management | Roles** (/admin/user/roles) and once created, will appear at the **Permissions** settings page. You may assign new roles to users by editing the user's account and checking the new roles. You can see all users on the site by visiting **Administer | User management | Users** (at /admin/user/user), where you will see links to edit their accounts.

When you first set up the Image module, two sizes are set up for your site: **Thumbnail** (at 100x100 pixels), and **Preview** (at a maximum of 640x640 pixels). The Thumbnail size is displayed when the image is shown as a teaser such as on the front page and on the gallery pages, and the Preview size is shown on the full page.

Though it may be convenient when first setting up a site, for many sites these defaults will probably not be adequate. You may change the sizes your images are displayed in by going to **Administer | Site Configuration | Images | Files and sizes** (at /admin/settings/image). On this page, you will see text fields for **Width**, **Height**, and **Link** in the **Image sizes** fieldset. Also, each size may be set to **Scale** or **Scale and crop**, which is the second option for creating exact-sized images. (There are settings available for the **Default image path** and **Maximum upload size** on the page as well.)

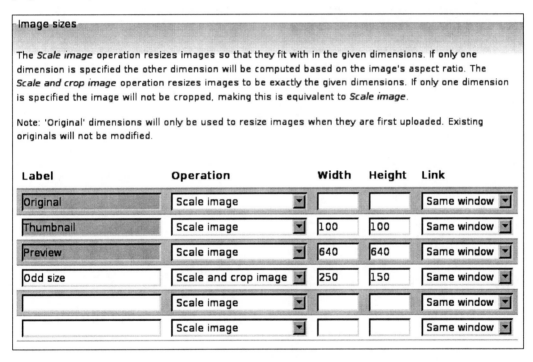

You may change the settings for your **Original, Thumbnail,** and **Preview** sizes here. If you have values for both width and height, then the resulting image will be resized to a maximum width by height (in pixels). If you enter only one value, then it will be scaled down exactly to that width or height with the other value changing appropriately to keep the same aspect ratio.

You may add more image sizes here as well. By default, only the **Thumbnail** and **Preview** sizes will be shown automatically on the site. But the other sizes will also be made available as links on the image node page. However, you will have access to those new sizes when theming your site. We will cover this later in the book.

The **Link** settings will configure the links shown at the bottom of the image node page. If set to **Same Window** and clicked on, the link will display the node page with the new size. If set to **New Window**, then the link will pop up as an image displayed in a new window. (As a technical note for innovative developers, these link elements will have CSS class elements applied, which could be useful when combined with jQuery to create pop ups with automatically-resized windows.)

Note that if you make a change to a size setting, any images you created before making the change will still have the old size. They will be recreated as needed before getting displayed, and you will receive a reminder. The first user to see a new size may receive a message stating something like, *Cool Pix thumbnail* **derivative image had a timestamp** (*Sun, 07/13/2008 - 17:09*) **that predates the last changes to the image size settings** (*Sun, 07/13/2008 - 17:44*)**. The derivatives will be rebuilt to regenerate it.** To force the system to resize the image files, you can also do this manually, by visiting the image node or gallery page that displays its thumbnail, by editing an image and checking the **Rebuild derivative images** box, or by going to **Administer | Content management | Content** (at /admin/content/node), selecting the images you wish to resize, and selecting **Rebuild image thumbnails** from the **Update options** drop-down.

Image Gallery Settings

You may change some basic gallery settings at **Administer | Site configuration | Images | Image gallery** (/admin/settings/image/image_gallery). These include how many images to display on a gallery page (by default 6), whether to display the **Posted by** information on those pages, and the **Image display sort order**.

```
┌─────────────────────────────────────────────────────────────┐
│  ┌─ Gallery settings ────────────────────────────────        │
│                                                               │
│    Images per page:                                           │
│    ┌──────┐                                                   │
│    │6     │                                                   │
│    └──────┘                                                   │
│    Sets the number of images to be displayed in a gallery page.│
│                                                               │
│    ┌─┐                                                        │
│    │ │  Display node info                                     │
│    └─┘                                                        │
│    Checking this will display the "Posted by" node information on the gallery pages.│
│                                                               │
│    Image display sort order:                                  │
│     ◉  Create date, newest first                              │
│     ○  Create date, oldest first                              │
│     ○  File name                                              │
│     ○  Image title                                            │
│                                                               │
└─────────────────────────────────────────────────────────────┘
```

Gallery Alternatives

As noted earlier, there are alternatives for using the **Image Gallery** module to display images. These options range from using add-ons that build onto Image's functionality, to full-blown packages that use their own system, to building your own gallery from scratch with existing tools.

Acidfree comes with more features than **Image Gallery**, and in fact builds on top of the **Image** module. It is designed to be simple to set up and use. However, it has not yet been upgraded for Drupal 6.

Gallery uses a library external to Drupal called **Gallery 2**, which has a thriving community of its own and offers features not seen in other options. This requires a third-party installation from `http://gallery.menalto.com/`. However, this will usually require learning another theming system apart from Drupal, if you do not want one of the themes provided out-of-the-box. Also, the images are not as well integrated into Drupal or supported by other modules.

You can also build your own gallery using a combination of modules. You might start by changing the theme of **Image Gallery**. Or you may create your own type of image node using a combination of the **CCK** and the **ImageField** modules, and wrapping it all up with **Views**. All of these techniques will be covered in the later chapters.

There are certainly other options available. If none of the options presented work best for your site, you would be served well by searching Drupal's forums and groups, and studying the contributed modules available to the community. The truly inspired ones are always welcome to join an existing project, helping to extend and improve the media-handling capabilities of Drupal.

A Brief Note about Image Toolkits

The **Image** module (as do other modules) uses a PHP Image toolkit to manipulate images such as for resizing and cropping. By default, the GD2 toolkit will be used when you install the **Image** module. This toolkit is compiled by default with PHP, and so is supported by most host providers.

You may wish to use **ImageMagick** instead, which must be compiled for PHP on your server. **ImageMagick** supports more image types such as GIF and PNG files. It also allows advanced image manipulation functions such as rotation and gradient creation, although at the time of this writing most of that is not being harnessed well by Drupal.

 To enable **ImageMagick**, first copy the `image.imagemagick.inc` file from `/sites/all/modules/image` to `/include`. (In both cases, these folders are relative to Drupal's root installation directory.)

After doing this, you will need to visit **Administer | Site configuration | Image toolkit** (at `/admin/settings/image-toolkit`) and select the new toolkit. Assuming everything goes well, you will see the **Version** and **Copyright** information for **ImageMagick**. (If not, then your server may not have ImageMagick installed and you will either need to contact your host or compile it yourself, or switch back to the default GD2 toolkit.) You can learn more about ImageMagick at `http://www.imagemagick.org`, and by searching for it at `Drupal.org`. Once you have done this, you may also want to install the **ImageMagick Advanced Options** module that is bundled with the **Image** module:

Image toolkit

Select an image processing toolkit:

○ GD2 image manipulation toolkit

◉ ImageMagick Toolkit.

ImageMagick Binary

ImageMagick is a standalone program used to manipulate images. To use it, it must be installed on your server and you need to know where it is located. If you are unsure of the exact path consult your ISP or server administrator.

Path to the "convert" binary: *

```
/usr/bin/convert
```

Specify the complete path to the ImageMagic convert binary. For example: /usr/bin/convert or C:\Program Files\ImageMagick-6.3.4-Q16\convert.exe

☐ Display debugging information

Checking this option will display the ImageMagick commands and ouput to users with the *administer site configuration* permission.

```
Version: ImageMagick 5.5.6 04/01/03 Q16 http://www.imagemagick.org
Copyright: Copyright (C) 2003 ImageMagick Studio LLC
```

ImageMagick Advanced Options

These settings let you control some of ImageMagick's more advanced options.

JPEG quality:

```
75
```
%

Define the image quality for JPEG manipulations. Ranges from 0 to 100. Higher values mean better image quality but bigger files. More information on -quality

Strip metadata from images at this size and below:

```
150x150
```

You may choose to strip all metadata, such as camera information and color profiles, from the processed images in order to reduce their file size. Please choose at what maximum size you want images to be stripped of their metadata. Example: "150x150". Enter "0x0" to disable this feature. This option requires ImageMagick 6.0.0 or higher. More information on -strip

Convert colorspace:

```
<None> ▾
```

This option lets you convert images to the specified colorspace. This will be overridden by the Color profile option, if used. More information on -colorspace

☑ Change image resolution to 72 ppi

If checked, this option will set the print resolution of the image to 72 pixels per inch, which is suitable for web use. This does not affect the pixel size or quality of the image. More information on -density

▷ Sharpening filter

▷ Color profile

There are other image toolkits available as well. The **Acidfree Albums** module uses another toolkit called **Imagick** (which makes use of the ImageMagick libraries, but does not fork its own process). This toolkit allows lossless JPEG rotation, which **Acidfree** uses when available.

Finally, there are other toolkits available to PHP that offer better, more, and/or different functionalities. These include Netpbm, ImLib2, and FreeImage. Netpbm is comprehensive, and supports conversion between image types. ImLib2 is faster than ImageMagick, but does not support as many file types. FreeImage is a binary library accessible from other languages besides PHP and is available across many operating systems.

Drupal 7 will make the support for various Image toolkits easier, moving the functionalities from include files to modules. Once this is in place, it will be easier to natively support more image-handling functions and allow contributed modules to offer more of the features editors would like to see on their sites.

If your server does not have any PHP image toolkit installed, you will see the error: **No image toolkit is currently enabled. Without one the image module will not be able to resize your images.** In this case, first go to **Administer | Site configuration | Image toolkit** (at `/admin/settings/image-toolkit`). Ideally, your server will at the very least have the built-in **GD2 toolkit** installed. If not, you will need to ask your hosting company to recompile PHP with the GD2 toolkit enabled, or move to another hosting company.

Teaser Thumbnails

Our next project requires us to use teaser thumbnails for articles. We have been hired by The Seedy Grapevine, a local social gossip column, to create an online version of its weekly rag. One of its requirements is to add an optional teaser image to its articles, which will display as a thumbnail on the front page and a larger image on the article page.

As is usually the case, there are many possible solutions to this need. But because it's not paying us much, and we want to just get the job done quickly, we're going to do the easiest thing we can. Yet its editors will be happy because the quick route is also easy for them to use. It's out of the box, and though there are certainly more complex solutions (often required for complex needs), our solution will harness the power of the **Image** module that we've already seen.

Image attach

The **Image attach** module is included in the **Image** download. Since we've already installed and configured that module, we just need to visit **Administer | Site building | Modules** (at /admin/build/modules) and activate the **Image attach** module.

This will allow us to attach image nodes to any other type of content. For the purpose of this project, we will use the **Story** type content, which is built-in and active by default on all Drupal sites. For a more complex solution, we would probably build our own type with multiple image fields (which we'll do in the next chapter). But we would still be able to use this module with those types, if it were the best solution.

Image attach Content Settings

To attach images to a content type, we must visit the settings page for that type. In this case, we'll go to **Administer | Content management | Content types | Story** (at /admin/content/node-type/story):

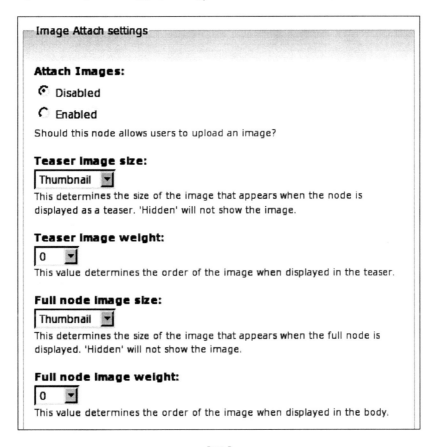

Now we just change the settings we need. Obviously, we'll first enable **Attach Images**. Leaving the **Teaser image size** at **Thumbnail**, we'll change the **Full node image size** to **Preview**.

The weights (from lowest to highest) determine where in the content the image will be displayed in relation to the body and fields (if using **CCK** fields) of the node type.

Attaching Images to Content

Now we are ready for our editors to actually begin attaching the images. As with images, you may wish users with an editor role to be able to create stories on the site by assigning that permission at **Administer | User management | Permissions** (at /admin/user/permissions). Users in this example must have both the permission to **create story content** and to **create image content**.

Putting on our editor hat, we go to **Create content | Create Story** (at /node/add/ story). We'll add a juicy title, the body content of our article, and then open the fieldset that reads **Attached images**:

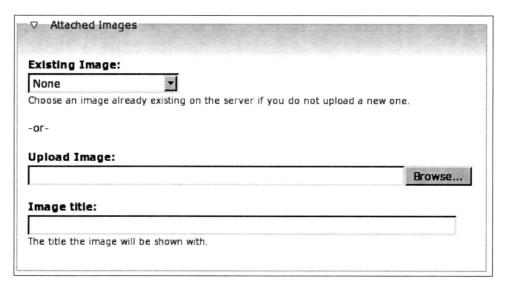

We can go ahead and insert an existing image that's been uploaded to the site from the **Existing Image** drop-down selector, or we can upload a new image directly from this form. In our example, we'll upload our new image here, hit **Save**, and see the new image magically float into our content!

Image Attach Rocks! View Edit

Wed, 11/14/2007 - 16:47 — aaron

Lorem ipsum dolor sit amet, consectetuer adipiscing elit. Vestibulum feugiat, risus vel aliquet elementum, quam augue pretium sem, euismod egestas erat erat sit amet enim. Vestibulum placerat pellentesque metus. Duis rutrum blandit purus. Praesent ante lectus, congue a, auctor ut, mollis in, massa. Mauris fringilla interdum nibh. Aliquam lobortis diam sit amet lectus. Quisque eu purus sit amet arcu tristique elementum. Quisque pulvinar. Morbi sit amet metus vel augue consectetuer vestibulum. Nullam vitae lectus. Pellentesque vehicula scelerisque quam. Nullam pharetra diam quis mi. Vestibulum ante ipsum primis in faucibus orci luctus et ultrices posuere cubilia Curae; Integer lobortis molestie sapien. Nunc ac ante in arcu accumsan tempor.

Ut accumsan dui vel enim. Proin interdum ante nec ipsum. Morbi id erat. Nunc non sapien. Praesent felis. Cras scelerisque, augue vitae sollicitudin bibendum, nisl ligula suscipit quam, id porttitor quam nunc in velit. Maecenas at nibh a dui pharetra aliquam. Fusce eu nibh. Suspendisse mi velit, commodo a, convallis vitae, hendrerit quis, nisl. Mauris in mi quis ipsum semper tristique. Cras laoreet mauris et erat. Fusce leo arcu, consequat id, tempor quis, fermentum at, sem. Cras venenatis interdum tortor. Ut urna nisl, fringilla eu, consequat non, iaculis vitae, erat. Duis fringilla nibh vitae libero. Mauris nunc.

Navigating back to our home page, we'll see the new image as a teaser thumbnail for our new story as well:

Image Attach Rocks!

Wed, 11/14/2007 - 16:47 — aaron

Lorem ipsum dolor sit amet, consectetuer adipiscing elit. Vestibulum feugiat, risus vel aliquet elementum, quam augue pretium sem, euismod egestas erat erat sit amet enim. Vestibulum placerat pellentesque metus. Duis rutrum blandit purus. Praesent ante lectus, congue a, auctor ut, mollis in, massa. Mauris fringilla interdum nibh. Aliquam lobortis diam sit amet lectus. Quisque eu purus sit amet arcu tristique elementum. Quisque pulvinar. Morbi sit amet metus vel augue consectetuer vestibulum. Nullam vitae lectus. Pellentesque vehicula scelerisque quam. Nullam pharetra diam quis mi.

Add new comment   Read more

Note that you may not want editors to be able to attach existing images to content. For instance, if you have a site with multiple uses of image nodes, such as with a gallery, it may get too confusing to keep them sorted. On the other hand, note also that image nodes created with **Image attach** will automatically be marked as not published and so they will not show up for users except as an attached image.

To disable the option to attach existing images, navigate to **Administer | Site configuration | Images | Image attach** (at `/admin/settings/image/image_attach`).

You may wish to change the placement of the attached image. For the most part, you'll need to change your theme's stylesheet to do this. The **Image attach** module automatically floats attached images to the right using its `image_attach.css` file. We'll learn more about overriding stylesheets in later chapters.

Images Embedded in Content

For our last example we are creating a high-powered blog, **Robot Watch**. We want the ability to paste images into the content. While we could certainly use the **Image attach** module with some success to achieve this, the limitations become apparent after use.

First, we are only allowed one attached image per node. That may be fine in some circumstances, but for our blog we want to be able to display several images per article in different places in the content. The next limitation is: attached images placed with **Image attach** will always be displayed in the same position. Finally, attached images will always have the same styles applied to them, meaning they will always float right (or left, or centered, or however the styles are defined).

We want to embed images inline within our content. We need to be able to have an image of a futuristic android at the top of a post, a bar graph of robotic industries in the third paragraph, and GIF animations of robots walking along the bottom of the page.

The multiple image issue might be taken care of by Drupal 6:

HTML

Before continuing, it's good to review an option that is built into Drupal. It is possible, if an editor knows how, to embed HTML directly into node content. As long as the input formats allow, you may manually insert images without the use of any contributed modules.

To do this, we would first need to use an **Input Format** that allows images in posts. By default, HTML is automatically scanned to remove images and other code before display. This is important to help deter spammers and to stop malicious code from being inserted by untrusted users.

If our user account has the permission to change the input format used by a post, we can change it underneath the text area of our story content. Permissions for input formats are controlled at **Administer | Site configuration | Input formats** (/admin/settings/filters). For this example, we will need to click on the **configure** link next to the **Full HTML** filter. Then, select any role that you wish to allow to the user of this filter. In most cases, you may not want to assign this filter to anonymous or authenticated users, reserving this capability only to your editors and administrators.

Once you've done this, your editors will be able to use the format with their content. By default, nodes will still be formated with the **Filtered HTML** format, which will strip out image tags. So we will still need to manually select the **Full HTML** format when entering images.

Now entering a new blog node, we type our snazzy title, write our insightful post in the body, and open the **Input Format** fieldset below the body text area, selecting **Full HTML** from the options.

When entering images directly as HTML, we have several options available. Firstly, we may directly link to an image outside our site such as `<img src="http://upload.wikimedia.org/wikipedia/en/8/8e/I_Robot_-_Runaround.jpg">`. Obviously, there are many reasons we probably don't want to do this such as the etiquette of not leeching from other servers, or the lack of control on the availability of that image.

Thus, we will probably want to host the image on our own server. In this case, we could simply upload an image directly to our `/files` directory, and link to it that way. We would then enter `<img src="/sites/example.com/files/robot-wars.jpg">` in our content.

However, our editors might not have FTP access to our servers, and so we might direct them to create image nodes and link directly to the images thus created. Image nodes automatically have a way to link to an image without needing to know the filename created: `/image/view/[nid]`, where `[nid]` is the node's nid that can be seen by examining the node's URL. In this case, we might have a link to `<img src="/image/view/392">`.

If you have many images in your `/files` directory that you would like to convert into image nodes, you can use the **Image Import** module that comes bundled with Image. This will import images in batches, which might be useful in a case such as this.

Image Assist

Unfortunately, we might have editors who don't understand HTML. Likewise, many editors will find this process tedious even if they know their way around HTML. Plus, hunting the nid for 30 images to insert into content might easily become unwieldy. In those cases, the solution of embedding HTML might be suboptimal.

The **Image Assist** module comes to our rescue. Available at `http://drupal.org/project/img_assist`, it will allow us to add new images with the click of a button and will display them where we want in the content.

After installing this module, you will also need to visit the Input Formats configuration page. Browse to **Administer | Site configuration | Input Formats** (at `/admin/settings/filters`) and click **configure** next to **Filtered HTML**. Alternatively, if you don't want anyone to be able to enter images, you might select another format, such as **Full HTML**, or even create a new format specifically for this purpose. However, that will require manually selecting the new format each time you add a node that you wish to embed images in.

Check the box next to **Inline images** underneath the **Filters** fieldset. After submitting this form, it's time to add a new story. Or in keeping with the example, we could add a new blog entry assuming we first activated the blog module that's built into Drupal.

Write two or three paragraphs in the Body text area. Now put your cursor at the beginning of the post, and click the button now showing at the bottom left of the text area:

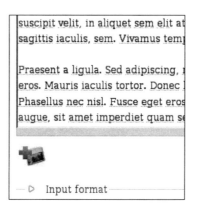

This will open a new window. If you already have image nodes on the site, then these will appear as thumbnails on this page. You may choose an existing image to embed or you may upload a new image:

If you upload a new image, you will next see a form that suspiciously looks like an image node submission form. In fact, that is exactly what it is. You will fill in these fields normally, entering a title, and a description for the body if desired.

When you submit this form, a new image node will be created. If you set a gallery for it, it will appear in the galleries. If you set it to promote to the front page, it will.

On the next page, you will have options for embedding this image into your original post. These options include drop-downs for the **Size**, **Alignment**, **Link**, and **Insert mode**:

The sizes will include any image sizes you've defined at the Image configuration screen (**Administer | Site configuration | Image**, at /admin/settings/image). The alignment will determine where to place the image: **left, right, center,** or **none. Left** and **right** will float the image in relation to the content, **center** will place it in the center of its content area, and **none** will place it inline to where you position it.

The **Link** selector will determine the behavior of the image. The default, **Not a link,** will simply place the image with no special behavior. Setting it to any other option will cause the image to act as a link when clicked on. This may be **Link to image page, Open in popup window,** or **Go to URL**. Selecting the last option will also ask for a URL to link the image to.

If you set the **Insert mode** text field to **HTML Code,** then the image will be inserted as HTML (for which you will need to select a filter that allows <img> tags such as Full HTML). But in most cases you will want to leave this at **Filter Tag,** which will insert the text in a special format that will be automatically converted before the image is displayed

After submitting this page, you will see this tag inserted into your content in a format similar to the following: [img_assist|nid=10|title=Asimo Look: New De sign|desc=|link=none|align=center|width=640|height=427]. You will be able to see the actual image after previewing or submitting the content:

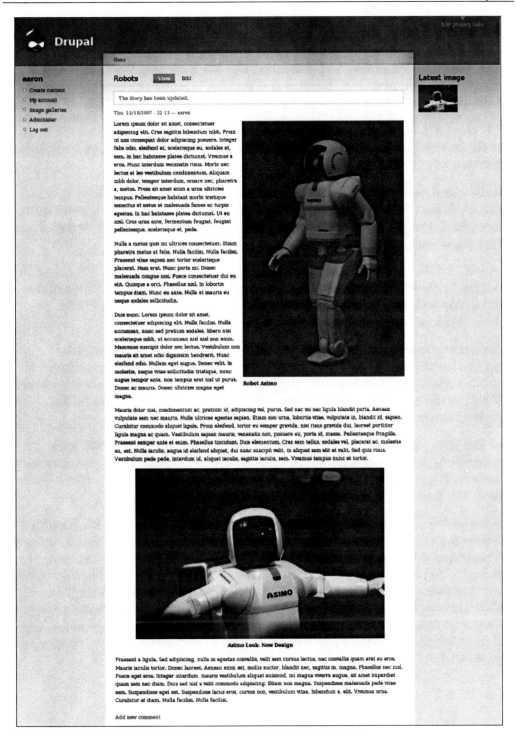

WYSIWYG

As a final note, an often-requested feature for editors is to use a WYSIWYG (What You See Is What You Get) editor for submitting content. There are several contenders for this, mainly **FCKeditor** and **TinyMCE**. As of this writing, the most feature-packed module with **Image Assist** support to boot is **TinyMCE**.

With **TinyMCE** installed on a site, text areas will be replaced (as needed) with a rich text editor, which will format the text so that you can see what it will look like before submitting or previewing.

Installing and configuring **TinyMCE** is not as straightforward as most contributed modules, in part because it is powered by a third-party editor. Because of licensing issues (don't worry, it's still open source), third-party software cannot be distributed from Drupal.org.

You will find the module at http://drupal.org/project/tinymce. You must also download **TinyMCE** from http://tinymce.moxiecode.com/. At the time of this writing, you will need version 3.1 (version 2.1 for Drupal 5), but you should double-check the requirements when installing the module.

After decompressing the download, you will need to put the tinymce folder from Moxiecode into the module's installation directory, as per the installation instructions included with the module. That folder will need to be named tinymce, and will be placed into the tinymce module folder resulting in /sites/all/modules/tinymce/tinymce.

You may also want to download and install **TinyMCE compressor PHP** from Moxiecode that's available on their download page, which will boost performance of the editor. The resulting tiny_mce_gzip.js and tiny_mce_gzip.php files will be placed into /sites/all/modules/tinymce/tinymce/jscripts/tiny_mce.

For **Image Assist** integration, you may also want to add a button within the editor by following the instructions for that module's installation. Note that this is optional, as **Image Assist** will work seamlessly with **TinyMCE** with its default behavior. Adding the following code will simply add a button to the editor, rather than using the button that appears just below the text area. If you wish to do this step, then in addition to copying the drupalimage folder from the **Image Assist** module directory to /sites/all/modules/tinymce/tinymce/jscripts/tiny_mce/plugins/, you will need to add the following code to /sites/all/modules/tinymce/plugin_reg.php, somewhere above the return statement:

```
$plugins['drupalimage'] = array();
$plugins['drupalimage']['theme_advanced_buttons1'] =
array('drupalimage');
$plugins['drupalimage']['extended_valid_elements'] = array('img[class|
src|border=0|alt|title|width|height|align|name]');
```

> Unfortunately, at the time of this writing, the **Drupal Image** plug-in for
> **TinyMCE** only worked for the Drupal 5 version of the module. This
> was because of differences in the required **TinyMCE** packages. There
> was a start towards adding support for Drupal 6, but it had not yet been
> completed. Hopefully by the time of this book's release, this feature will
> again be available. Please check the **Image Assist** module's installation
> instructions when installing the plug-in, deferring to those when they
> differ from the given instructions.

After uploading all these files to your site and making any optional code changes,
you will be able to install and configure **TinyMCE**. As usual, first go to **Administer
| Site building | Modules** (at /admin/build/modules) and activate the **TinyMCE**
module. Also make certain that your editors (and any other user roles you wish) may
use TinyMCE, at **Administer | User management | Permissions** (at /admin/user/
permissions). This step is necessary, even if you only wish for the User 1 super-
administrator account to use the text editor as **TinyMCE** profiles are role-based.

Next you will set up at least one profile for editing use by browsing to **Administer |
Site configuration | TinyMCE settings** (at /admin/settings/tinymce) and clicking
create a profile. In the **Basic Setup** fieldset, add the name of this profile, which we'll
arbitrarily call Editor, and enable the role(s) you wish to have access to. Note that
you may have multiple profiles, so that only Editors will have an **image** button and
authenticated users will not, for instance.

In this case, roles will have all the buttons from combined profiles for which they have access:

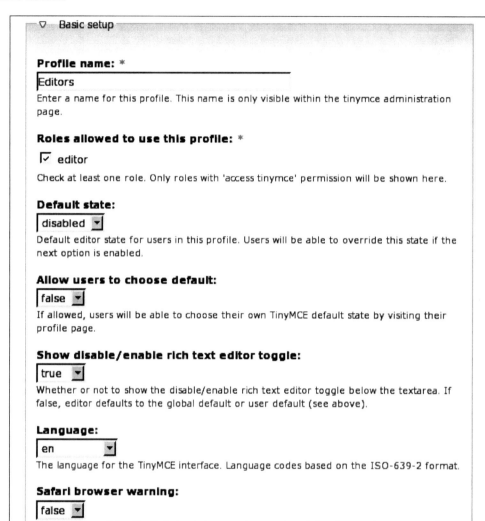

If you enable the default state using the Drupal 5 version, be aware that editing a node with PHP code will result in **TinyMCE** erasing that code. This is a limitation of **TinyMCE version 2.1**, and your only options at this time are to disable the editor while entering PHP in node content or using the third-party **PHP Plugin** available from the **TinyMCE SourceForge** project page at http://sourceforge.net/projects/tinymce/.

For now, we'll leave the options in the **Visibility** fieldset alone. Here you would specify the pages where fieldsets need to be replaced with **TinyMCE** editors. The default is for node, comment, and user profile text areas, which is fine in most cases.

The fun begins with the **Buttons and plugins** fieldset. Check the buttons you want to appear here for editors. As you can see, there are a lot of bells and whistles available, from the expected bold and italics to blockquotes and images to spell checking and text directionality. It is important to note that many of the buttons will not actually display text as we desire without changing our input formats at **Administer | Site configuration | Input formats** (/admin/settings/filters):

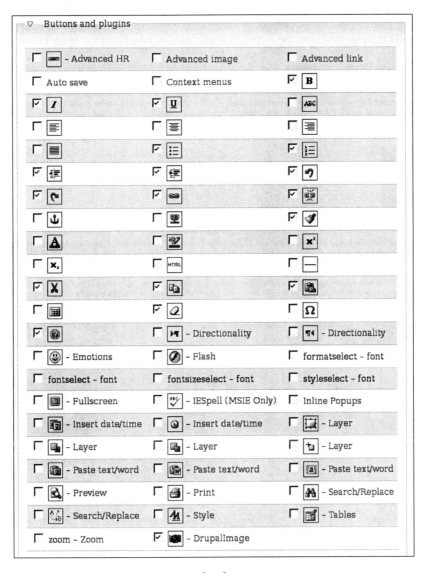

The settings shown here are suggested, but you may wish to experiment and set them according to the needs of your site. The **DrupalImage** icon at the bottom is different than the Image icon near the top, and it is what you will use for **Image Assist**. It is only available if you've followed the steps outlined for that plug-in. (The earlier icon is for inserting remote image URLs.)

Your profile will work now when you click **Create profile**, although you may wish to peruse the other options first. Specifically, you may want to set **Verify HTML** under **Cleanup and output** to **True** and depending on the complexity of your theme's stylesheet, you may need to set the **Editor CSS** under the **CSS** fieldset to **tinyMCE default**. (Sometimes, the theme's stylesheet will make the **TinyMCE** editor look odd. Technically, it is loading its own page within an IFrame, which means that it loads its own stylesheet independently of the containing page.)

Body:

Mauris tincidunt consequat est. Suspendisse rhoncus justo. Cras id risus. Ut aliquet posuere libero. Nam aliquet tortor at turpis elen Nam a lacus at leo pulvinar commodo. Pellentesque habitant morbi tristique senectus et netus et malesuada fames ac turpis eges pede, auctor et, placerat et, bibendum quis, quam. Pellentesque vel diam eget leo condimentum condimentum. Donec sagittis nec Suspendisse at sapien. Aenean id mauris at diam rhoncus tincidunt. Nulla euismod magna vitae elit. Etiam tempus facilisis nunc. In metus. Nam ut lorem vitae nisi pharetra semper.

**Zebra in South Africa:** A beautiful zebra. Made in Sabi Sand Private Game Reserve, South Africa. Photo b

Cras nec nisi ac lorem gravida sagittis. Ut porttitor turpis vel mauris. Phasellus eget lacus. Integer cursus auctor urna. In vulputate, ultrices, lectus nisi euismod nunc, non mollis dui nisi at sapien! Donec lectus. Pellentesque ut odio vel magna posuere vehicula. Ut l imperdiet nec, convallis non, pulvinar eget, massa. Nunc id lacus ut erat tincidunt pretium. Nullam arcu mi, pretium in, dapibus ac; lectus. Phasellus tortor neque, vestibulum a, tristique at, venenatis pretium, leo!

Mauris orci arcu; hendrerit ac, sollicitudin eget, commodo quis; eros. Integer viverra nibh vestibulum turpis. Nam euismod. Ut susci Nullam dictum, est a posuere lacinia, nibh tortor sodales sem, non tincidunt turpis est ac diam. Nullam leo. Cum sociis natoque per dis parturient montes, nascetur ridiculus mus. Donec tincidunt, eros a sollicitudin volutpat, mi ipsum vehicula diam, non consectetu pede. Curabitur aliquam. Aenean nec augue vitae lorem dictum molestie? Maecenas vel orci in nisl consequat vestibulum. Duis ve Vestibulum ante ipsum primis in faucibus orci luctus et ultrices posuere cubilia Curae; Fusce accumsan? Integer ut ante. Sed velit? fermentum sem ac metus? Aliquam a neque.

B *I* <u>U</u>

Path: p » span.inline inline-right

disable rich-text

Your node text areas will now be replaced with the **TinyMCE** plug-in, as just seen. Inline images, entered using the camera button for **Image Assist**, will be displayed with a small thumbnail version within the form element along with the various buttons for a WYSIWYG display.

WYSIWYG Alternatives

There are other WYSIWYG modules available for Drupal as well, although **TinyMCE** is arguably the most popular and one of the more developed. You are encouraged to explore them, particularly if you are unsatisfied with the performance of **TinyMCE**. Károly Négyesi (chx) wrote an overview of the current state of rich text editors for Drupal at `http://drupal4hu.com/node/144` and reading that may be a good start.

Summary

In this chapter we have learned how to create image galleries, attach images to our node content, and insert images inline within the content. We used the **Image** module and its related **Image Gallery**, to easily create a full-featured gallery that works right out of the box. Enabling **Image attach** allowed us to associate image nodes created with the Image module to specific content types such as **Articles** or **Blog** entries. Finally, **Image Assist**, with its optional WYSIWYG support for **TinyMCE**, offered an easy way to create and attach inline images to our content.

In the next chapter, we will explore some more advanced techniques for using images in our sites such as creating image fields for our custom content types.

3
Developing for Images

Developers often face the difficult task of translating their clients' needs into a multimedia-rich web application. Although in the previous chapter we discussed several powerful options that may be used, they will not always suffice. Often, the client will need various images displayed in various locations, depending on various functions. They may want images to be cropped before resizing. Or they may wish to embed images from an external image provider such as Flickr.

We will look at several use cases in this chapter, each of which will explore new options for displaying images. By the end of this chapter, we will have a firm groundwork for storing and displaying images in nearly any configuration you may desire.

Image Node: The Traditional Method

The previous chapter explored Images as nodes fairly comprehensively. Before deciding to go with a technique explored here, it might be worth first reviewing the options available with the **Image module** and its contributed modules such as **Image attach** and **Image Gallery**.

Some of the modules examined later, such as **ImageField**, might provide more flexibility. They currently provide their own engines for the storage and display of images, duplicating code or functionality where necessary. This sometimes makes the modules incompatible. For instance, if you create a node with an **Image Field**, it will be inaccessible to **Image Gallery**, requiring you to configure your own gallery perhaps using the **Views** module. In some cases, you may have no choice. In other cases, you may actually be creating more work for yourself.

Multiple Images

We'll start with a fairly involved requirement. Our client, Mr. Bob's Gadgets and Gizmos, wants to create a gallery of items for sale. The gallery will have a thumbnail that shows up on product listing pages. He also wants a larger thumbnail to display in a **Featured Gadget** block. Finally, each product will have the option to display several images on its page.

We review our options and first note that we don't want to use **Image nodes** for our product pages; each product requires specific information with more complex requirements than just a simple node. Besides, Mr. Bob is already using the **Image node** type and its **Image Gallery** module for posting pictures of his pet Pekingese.

We might just use **Image Attach** (also part of the **Image** package) for this situation: At the time of this writing, we can't attach multiple images. However, there is some code in the module to create a framework for this, which is in the to-do list. So by the time you read this, that module might just be the perfect fit.

However, even after seeing if Mr. Bob would like to sponsor that feature for the module, he clarifies that he wants the image that shows up in the **Featured Gadget** block to be a different image than what shows up on the teasers. So our needs are more complex than what that solution would allow anyway.

ImageField: Flexible, Powerful, Useful

So we'll look at **CCK** and then learn about its related **ImageField**. **CCK** will allow us to define new fields to store information and **ImageField** will attach images to nodes as specific fields.

This seems to be the perfect combination, although we'll also need to make use of the **ImageCache** and **Views** modules to polish it off. Additionally, **ImageField** requires the **FileField** to be installed and enabled (from `http://drupal.org/project/filefield`). We'll be making a heavy use of **FileField** in later chapters, by the way. Finally, we also need to install the **Token** module from `http://drupal.org/project/token`.

If you haven't already, enable both the **CCK** and **ImageField** modules by browsing to **Administer | Site building | Modules** (at `/admin/build/modules`). You'll also need to enable the **FileField**, **Token**, and **FileField Tokens** modules.

We're now going to create a new content type for our products. We'll need to store the following information for each product: **Product Name**, **Description**, **Teaser Thumbnail**, **Featured Gadget Image**, and **Gadget Images**.

Browse to **Administer | Content management | Content types | Add content type**
(at /admin/content/types/add) and enter the name of our new type, **Gadget**,
next to both **Name** and **Type**. On this screen, **Name** refers to what editors will see
when entering content of this type and **Type** is how it will be known internally to
Drupal. Thus, though they may often be the same, **Type** may not contain spaces
or other special characters, resulting in type names such as **news_article** and
slideshow_image.

The **Description** will display on the **Create content** page (at /node/add). After
entering a brief description, we'll rename **Title** to **Product Name**, and **Body** to
Description. Before submitting this page, make sure the other settings are what we
need: whether to automatically promote a node to the front page, enabling/disabling
comments, and so on. Leave **Attach Images** disabled since we'll be setting up our
custom image fields rather than using **Image Attach**.

After clicking **Save content type**, our new **Gadget** node type will appear on the
Content types administration page. We could actually begin creating new gadgets,
although we wouldn't have images yet.

So from the resulting screen at **Administer | Content management | Content types**
(admin/content/types), we'll click on the **edit** link in the **Gadget** operations.

There are now new menu items available on the tabs for this page. We need to click
on the **Add field** tab, which will bring us to /admin/content/node-types/gadget/
add_field. If we had already defined fields on other types, those existing fields
would appear in a drop-down, allowing us to redefine fields for multiple types.

For instance, we could have a **Node Reference** field that could refer to our gadgets
that could be reused for **Blog entries**, **News releases**, and **Article** content types. On
the other hand, we might want a particular **Image Field** that would be required with
only one image allowed, and another that is not required but allows for multiple
images. In that case, we wouldn't reuse that field.

Our first field will be the **Teaser Thumbnail**. Firstly, enter **teaser_thumbnail** for the
Field name, which will set the machine-readable name as **field_teaser_thumbnail**.
This is how the field is known to Drupal and we'll use that when referring to the
field in code.

Now, enter **Teaser Thumbnail** for the human-readable **Label**. Next, select **Image** for the **Field type** and click the **Continue** button:

Create new field

Field name: *

field_ |teaser_thumbnail

The machine-readable name of the field. This name cannot be changed later! The name will be prefixed with 'field_' and can include lowercase unaccented letters, numbers, and underscores. The length of the name, including the prefix, is limited to no more than 32 letters.

Label: *

|Teaser Thumbnail

A human-readable name to be used as the label for this field in the *Article* content type.

Field type: *

|Image ▼|

The type of data you would like to store in the database with this field.

You'll then see a similar screen, with the exception of a new selection drop-down, **Widget** type. Press **Continue** again.

Some field types have multiple widgets, which decide how to determine information when creating new content using the field such as with a text field or radio buttons. Images have only a **Widget type** of **Image**, which will be a file-upload text field.

Create new field

Field name:

field_teaser_thumbnail

The machine-readable name of the field. This name cannot be changed.

Label: *

Teaser Thumbnail

A human-readable name to be used as the label for this field in the *Article* content type.

Field type:

Image ▼

The type of data you would like to store in the database with this field. This option cannot be changed.

Widget type: *

Image ▼

The type of form element you would like to present to the user when creating this field in the *Article* content type.

Widget Field Settings

The next settings for our widget influence the display and storage of the field. We determine what kind and size of images to accept, where to store them, and other related options, as we'll see.

The top section of these settings is specific to this content type. We may share this field with other content types, and override them as and when needed.

First we see the **Help text**, which is displayed to editors when uploading images. Next are the **Permitted upload file extensions**. The default of `jpg jpeg png gif` is suitable in most cases. We could easily leave the **Maximum** and **Minimum resolution for Images**, as we'll resize them dynamically later. In fact, we could set both to our desired 80x80 and be done with it in this case. However, we're thinking of the future when we may want our teasers to be of a larger size. So, we'll set the minimum to 80x80 and leave the maximum value alone:

Gadget settings

These settings apply only to the *Teaser Thumbnail* field as it appears in the *Gadget* content type.

Help text:

This image will be used to represent this gadget in various listings throughout the site. It will be scaled and cropped to 80x80, so choose a suitable image for this.

Instructions to present to the user below this field on the editing form.

Permitted upload file extensions.:

jpg jpeg png gif

Extensions a user can upload to this field. Seperate extensions with a space and do not include the leading dot.

Maximum resolution for Images:

0

The maximum allowed image size expressed as WIDTHxHEIGHT (e.g. 640x480). Set to 0 for no restriction. If a larger image is uploaded, it will be resized to reflect the given width and height.

Minimum resolution for Images:

80x80

The minimum allowed image size expressed as WIDTHxHEIGHT (e.g. 640x480). Set to 0 for no restriction. If an image that is smaller than these dimensions is uploaded it will be rejected.

— ▷ File size restrictions ——————————————————————

— ▷ Path settings ————————————————————————————

— ▷ Title text settings ————————————————————————

— ▷ ALT text settings ————————————————————————

An important thing to know when working with **Image Field** is that it does not have different sizes available as **Image** nodes created with the **Image** module do. We'll need to use the **ImageCache** module to give us this kind of control, which we'll cover in the next section.

Opening the **File size restrictions** section, we see a **Maximum upload size per file** and **per node**. This can be invaluable when allowing user submitted images to counteract possible bloat on your file system. However, since these images will only be uploaded by our trusted editors, we'll leave the settings alone for now:

▽   File size restrictions

Limits for the size of files that a user can upload. Note that these settings only apply to newly uploaded files, whereas existing files are not affected.

Maximum upload size per file:

Specify the size limit that applies to each file separately. Enter a value like "512" (bytes), "80K" (kilobytes) or "50M" (megabytes) in order to restrict the allowed file size. If you leave this this empty the file sizes will be limited only by PHP's maximum post and file upload sizes.

Maximum upload size per node:

Specify the total size limit for all files in field on a given node. Enter a value like "512" (bytes), "80K" (kilobytes) or "50M" (megabytes) in order to restrict the total size of a node. Leave this empty if there should be no size restriction.

The **File path** will create a subdirectory of the /files folder. This can be useful for organizing photos, when examining them with the FTP to give a recognizable path for the photo URL and to reduce filename collisions. Note that when photos of the same filename are uploaded, the conflicting filename will be appended with a unique number, so this is usually not a problem. Additionally, we can use tokens here, which will dynamically be replaced with a specific value as a file is uploaded. For instance, [uid] would be replaced with the author's unique identifying number.

For this example we will set the **File path** to `images/teaser_thumbnail/[user]`, which will create folders on the fly for newly uploaded images such as `images/teaser_thumbnail/aaron` or `images/teaser_thumbnail/bob`. This will make it easier to manage our file assets later by automatically sorting images in the file system for the editors who will be uploading them:

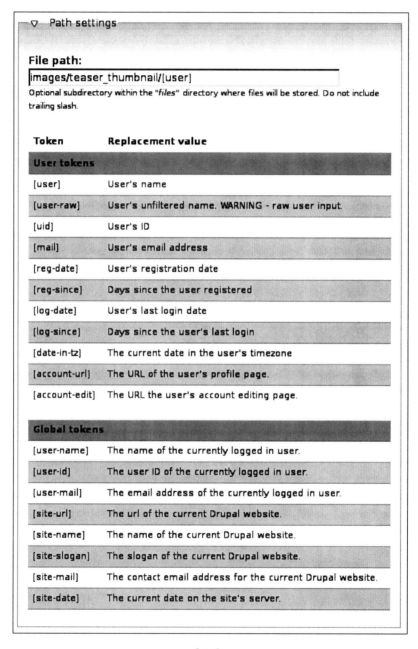

Again, we can use tokens for our **Default Title** and **ALT text** fields, which appear on our image tool tips, and for web text readers. We'll leave this alone as we can change that on an individual basis when needed:

▽   Title text settings

☐ Enable custom title text
Enable user input title text for images.

Default Title text:

This value will be used as the image title by default.

Token	Replacement value
Global tokens	
[user-name]	The name of the currently logged in user.
[user-id]	The user ID of the currently logged in user.
[user-mail]	The email address of the currently logged in user.
[site-url]	The url of the current Drupal website.
[site-name]	The name of the current Drupal website.
[site-slogan]	The slogan of the current Drupal website.
[site-mail]	The contact email address for the current Drupal website.
[site-date]	The current date on the site's server.

▽   ALT text settings

☐ Enable custom alternate text
Enable user input alternate text for images.

Default ALT text:

This value will be used for alternate text by default.

Token	Replacement value
Global tokens	
[user-name]	The name of the currently logged in user.
[user-id]	The user ID of the currently logged in user.

Global Settings

Finally, in our field's **Global settings**, we can set whether a field is **Required**, the allowed **Number of values**, and whether or not to **Always list files**. These settings will affect this particular image field, regardless of what content type uses it, as opposed to the previous settings that may be overridden on a case-by-case basis.

When required, attempting to submit content without uploading our thumbnail image will result in a validation error that will require the editor to upload an image before continuing.

If we changed the **Number of values** setting, we would be allowed to upload more than one image to a single node. This could be up to 10, or unlimited, according to the number selected.

If we check the **Always list files** box, then images will always be displayed with the node. Otherwise, the editor uploading them gets to determine that for each individual node:

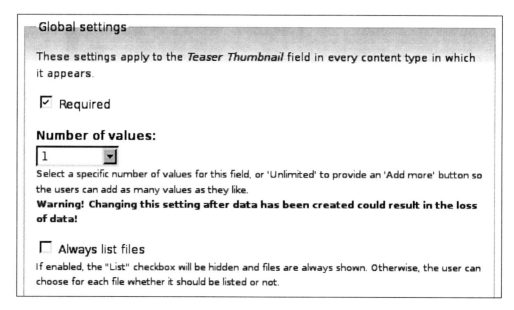

Leaving the other settings alone, let's set our **Teaser Thumbnail** to **Required** and click **Save field** settings, which will bring us to the Gadget's **Manage fields** tab.

Create a new field called **Gadget Images** by again clicking on **Add field**. As our last field, this will be an **Image**. But in addition to this, we'll also allow up to four values. Leave all the **Widget settings** as they are (unless we want to add some help text or group our field, and/or to set the **File path** to a custom value). Again, check the **Always list files** box.

Finally, we'll create one more image field named **Featured Gadget Image** (which will be known to the computer as **field_featured_gadget_image**). We'll leave the **Required** box unchecked and the **Number of values** at one, but check the **Always list files** box. We won't feature just any gadget as the thumbnail, we'll only want to display a single image here.

Managing Fields

On a content type's **Manage fields** page, we'll see a good overview of our fields. Here we can change the placement of our fields ensuring that, for instance, an image is displayed before the body or fields are grouped together. To change the order of fields, simply click and drag the handle to the left of a field to move it to another location:

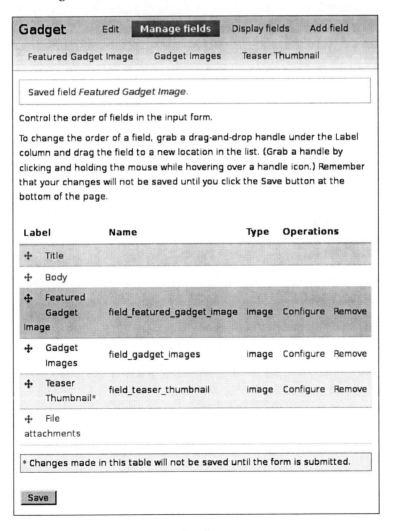

The **Manage fields** screen may be used to navigate to and edit existing fields by clicking on the **Configure** link next to a field, or from the tabs above. You can also remove fields from this screen as well, with the **Remove** link.

If you have the **Fieldgroup** module active on your site, you may group fields together as well, creating a new group with the **Add group** tab from this page. A group created in this way will become an option from the **Group** column of this page, or from the **Display in group** option on a field's configuration page.

Press the **Save** button to save the placement changes.

Creating Custom Content

Let's go ahead and create a gadget by browsing to **Create content** and clicking on the **Gadget** type (/node/add/gadget).

The following screenshot is shown in two parts.
Part one:

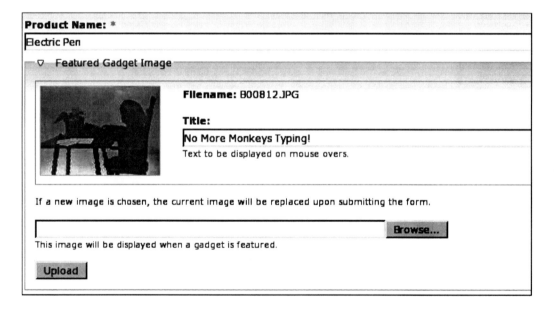

Part two:

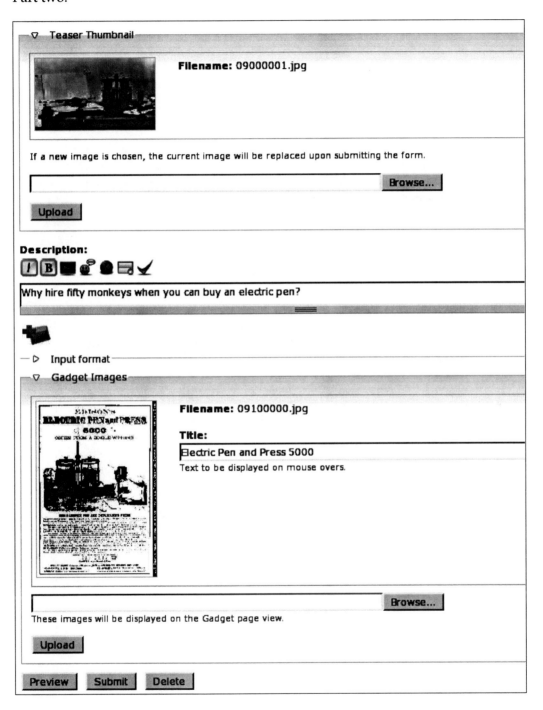

When entering or editing content with image fields, you will have a **Browse** button to select a file to upload. Then, you may **Preview** or **Submit** the post as usual or optionally **Upload** an individual image before continuing. As seen in this screenshot, once you've uploaded an image, you will have the opportunity to add a **Title** or **Alt tag** (if provided by the field definition). Additionally, if you wish to upload more than one image in a field that provides for multiple values, then you will need to press the **Upload** button first.

Display Fields

When we examine our new gadget, we will unfortunately not see any photos. They are listed (assuming we checked the **List box** earlier) with links to the actual photos. However, in nearly every circumstance, this is not acceptable:

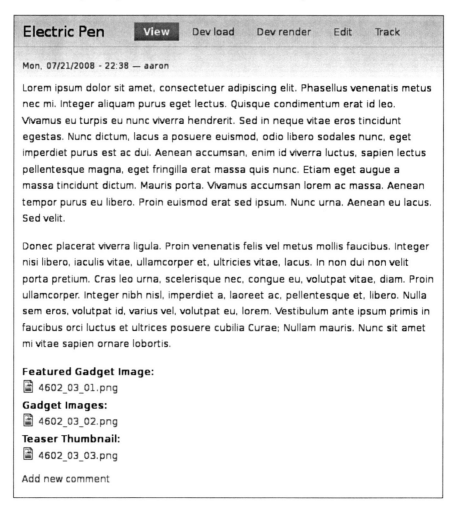

Though the default display for **Image Fields** is unsuitable for our purposes, the **CCK** makes it easy for us to customize the content display. We can determine whether to display an image or not on a per-field basis. We'll do this now by browsing to the **Gadget | edit | Display fields** tab (at `/admin/content/ node-type/gadget/display`):

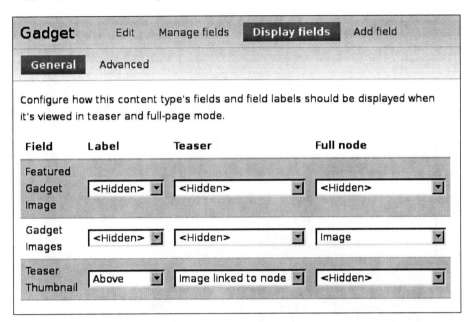

We will hide the labels for the **Featured Gadget Image** and the **Teaser Thumbnail** by selecting **<Hidden>**. For this example, we'll keep the label for the multiple **Gadget Images** above the display.

All images but the **Teaser Thumbnail** will be hidden when displayed as a **Teaser**, and only **Gadget Images** will be displayed on the **Full node** page mode. We do this by setting them to **Image linked to node** and **Image** respectively, and selecting **<Hidden>** for the other image fields.

After submitting this page, we can go back to the front page (assuming we promote our gadgets to the front page) and see the teaser formatted properly, and likewise for our full page:

Block Views

We've hinted at a new block for our **Featured Gadget Image**. That block will feature a random image that's been marked sticky by our editors. Let's create that now. We'll need to make sure our **Views** module is active, which was covered in the first chapter. Assuming the module has been enabled, go to **Administer | Site building | Views** (at /admin/build/views) and click the **Add** tab (which brings you, appropriately enough, to /admin/build/views/add).

Name this view **featured_gadget**. This is the machine name, and may not have spaces or punctuation. You may also enter a brief description for the administration page to help differentiate the new view from others. You might also want to give it a tag such as Gadgets:

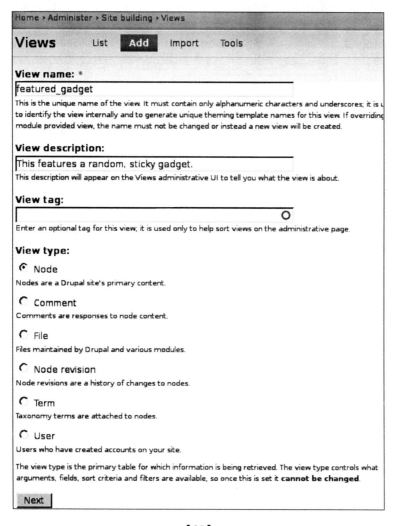

After clicking **Next**, you will be at the **Defaults** for the view. We'll just add a **Block** display using the drop-down selector and pressing **Add display** on the left, and edit the details there. Adding options here will also affect the defaults, if we add other displays to the view later.

Give the block a **Title** of **Featured Gadget** and enter **1** for **Items to display**.

Fields are used only with List and Table views. They determine what will be displayed for nodes selected for the view, rather than depending only on a teaser or full page view.

Now we'll add a couple of fields by pressing the **+** button to the right of **Fields**. Add our image by selecting **Image: field_featured_gadget_image** from the resulting drop-down and pressing the **Add** button:

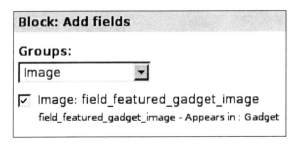

After pressing **Add**, you'll have a chance to select the **Format** of the field: Select **Image linked to node** and press **Update**:

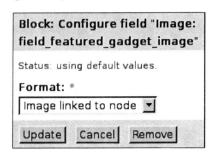

After that submits, do the same for **Node: Title** by checking **Link this field to its node** and blanking out its **Label** before updating.

Now, **Filters**. We use filters to determine which nodes to display in our block. Add two filters, **Node: Sticky** and **Node: Type** by pressing the **+** button next to **Filters** and checking those two boxes. For the **Value** of **Node: Type**, select **Gadget**; this will ensure that only gadgets are chosen.

Lastly, select **Global: Random** for the **Sort Criteria**.

After saving these changes, you will have a new block on the **Blocks** administration page (**Administer | Site building | Blocks | List** at /admin/build/block/list). Select the **Right sidebar** region for the block and press **Save blocks**.

Since we are only featuring nodes that have been marked as **Sticky**, we need to enter a new gadget with that setting. Enter a new gadget at **Create content | Create Gadget** (/node/add/gadget), and check the **Sticky at top of lists** box in the **Publishing options** field set.

After submitting this (and a couple of more for testing purposes), a random gadget will be featured.

Resizing and Cropping

You've probably noticed by now a limitation of the **Image Field** that images can't be resized as easily as they can be with the **Image** module. You can set a maximum image resolution, but what about multiple image sizes? Such a simple feature, you think?

Not to worry. The **ImageCache** module comes to our rescue. It allows not only resizing, but also scaling and cropping, or any combination of these actions. In addition, there is no limit to the number of image size rules that can be created.

So images only need to be resized and/or cropped once. Images dynamically created by the module are cached in the /files directory, hence the module's name. Of course, the **Image** module does this as well. The main difference is the options that may be applied and, more importantly, that they may be applied to any image type in the file system, whether to **Image** nodes, attached images, or **Image Fields**.

To demonstrate how to use this module, we'll take the case of Fishtopia, an imaginary encyclopedia of aquatic vertebrates of the world.

The Fishtopian Society wants to have articles about fish, with a single image that may be uploaded to be used as a teaser image, featured image, and main article image. Additionally, they want to have gallery images that display as thumbnails, which can be clicked for a larger image.

For this example we'll create a new content type, **Fish Article**, with two image fields. We already know how to do this, so this can be an exercise of creativity. Create the new type from **Administration | Content management | Content types | Add content type** (at /admin/content/types/add). Add two image fields, naming a single image field as **Main Image** and an image field with multiple images as **Gallery Images**.

ImageCache

The following screenshot demonstrates the capabilities of the **ImageCache** module. As you can see, the module allows for a number of server-side image manipulations, including scaling, resizing, and cropping images. These may further be combined, as we'll see in a moment:

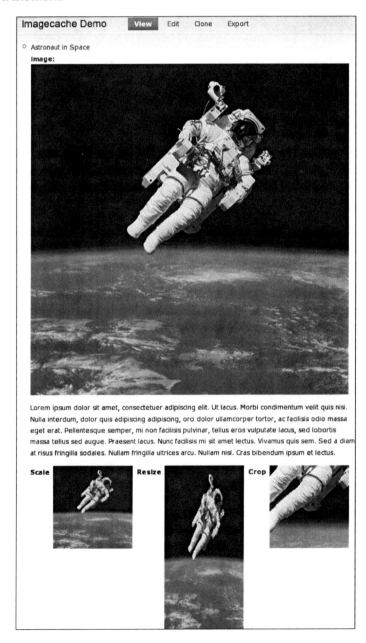

The **ImageCache** module needs to be enabled for the next task, possibly setting access rules for administrators to continue. It can be found at `http://drupal.org/project/imagecache`.

Once you've set that up, go to **Administer | Site building | Imagecache | Add new preset** (at `/admin/build/imagecache/add`). You will create **Presets** here, which once created may be applied to any image in Drupal's file system.

Our first preset will be for **fish_article_thumbnails**. Go ahead and enter **fish_article_thumbnail** as the **Preset Namespace** (which can't have spaces) and press **Create New Preset** now:

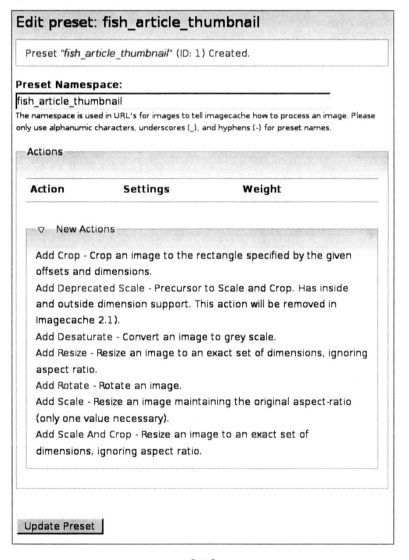

The client has requested that these images be squared off and cropped down to 150x150. In their wireframes, they have designated this size for the **Main Image** when it's displayed as a teaser, and for the **Gallery Image** thumbnails when viewing the article page.

Add a new action for **Add Scale and Crop**, press **Update preset**, and set the **Width** and **Height** to 150 (pixels):

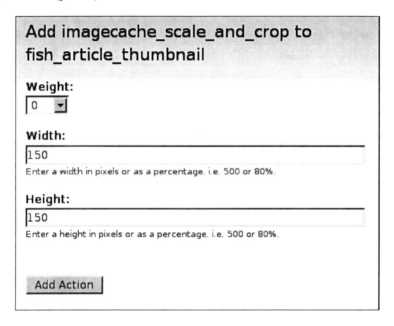

You now have this **ImageCache** preset available for your images.

Go to **Administer | Content management | Fish Article | Display fields** (at /admin/content/node-type/fish-article/display) and select **fish_article_ thumbnail** as link-to node for the **Main Image**'s teaser, and **Image** for **Full node**. Select **<Hidden>** for the **Gallery Images** teaser, and **fish_article_thumbnail** for its **Full node** display.

You may also want to change the order in which images are displayed. For this example we'll put the **Gallery Images** below the article body. Go back to the **Manage Fields** tab of the **Fish Article** content type page (at /admin/content/node-type/ fish-article/fields), and drag and place **Gallery Images** below the **Main Image**.

Submit that, enter some test Fish Articles, and marvel at how easy that was:

Grouper   **View**   Edit

The *Fish Article* has been updated.

Sun, 12/16/2007 - 18:20 — aaron

Main Image:

Lorem ipsum dolor sit amet, consectetuer adipiscing elit. Aliquam faucibus malesuada orci. Nulla ac ligula. Suspendisse adipiscing hendrerit nisl. Sed felis. Ut elementum purus id orci. Nulla aliquam nunc eleifend elit vestibulum vehicula. Morbi sodales vestibulum mi. Etiam condimentum, ante sit amet facilisis malesuada, felis tellus tincidunt elit, vel porta dolor ante vitae urna. Ut imperdiet leo non purus. Maecenas suscipit. Aliquam rhoncus. Nunc in neque eget turpis condimentum tempor. Maecenas feugiat neque non libero. Sed interdum purus nec nulla. Vivamus sit amet enim. Quisque quis magna. Donec nec erat nec est dictum consequat.

Gallery Images:

Add new comment   3

Third-Party Images

A recent phenomenon on the Internet has been the embedded sharing of images and other media from third-party providers. For example, Flickr is a site that allows users to upload photos for display, and further allows those photos to be embedded directly into another user's blog or other site.

Historically, this type of media sharing was discouraged, in part because of the strain on web servers when multiple sites might use the same image. Now, due to the increase of available bandwidth and the revenue available from advertising and other means, many sites actually encourage sharing images and media from their servers.

Flickr and other third-party image providers usually include instructions for users to include an image in their own blog, which may involve pasting HTML into a post, registering a blog with the site, or other methods. Although this is a possible solution for editors, there is an easier way for Drupal users.

Embedded Media Field

The **Embedded Media Field** module has evolved as a way to consolidate some of the larger third-party media providers. The last couple of years have seen an exponential growth in sharing media content between sites. **Embedded Media Field** tries to make managing this much easier for editors.

Now to include a third-party image in their content, an editor simply needs to copy and paste the URL of a post. Assuming the provider is supported by the module, **Embedded Media Field** will parse the URL or embed the code, automatically determine the provider, and appropriately display the image. **Embedded Media Field** handles video and audio as well, which we'll explore in later chapters.

First, install this module and its included **Embedded Image Field** from the project page at `http://drupal.org/project/emfield`. For Flickr, which we'll be using for this example, you'll also need to apply for and enter a **Flickr Developer's API key** before images may be displayed. Do this by following the directions from the **Embedded Media Field** configuration page (by browsing to **Administer | Content types | Embedded Media Field configuration** at `/admin/content/emfield`), and opening the **Embedded Image Field** section and **Flickr** underneath its **Providers** subsection:

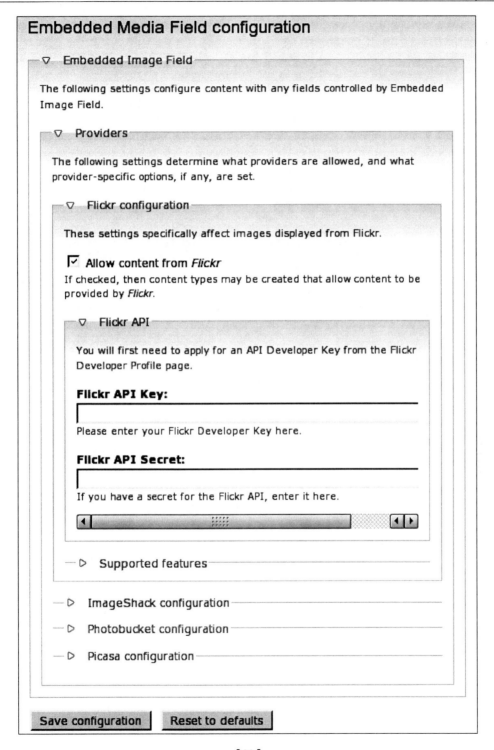

Embedded Media Field configuration

▽ Embedded Image Field

The following settings configure content with any fields controlled by Embedded Image Field.

▽ Providers

The following settings determine what providers are allowed, and what provider-specific options, if any, are set.

▽ Flickr configuration

These settings specifically affect images displayed from Flickr.

☑ **Allow content from *Flickr***

If checked, then content types may be created that allow content to be provided by *Flickr*.

▽ Flickr API

You will first need to apply for an API Developer Key from the Flickr Developer Profile page.

Flickr API Key:

Please enter your Flickr Developer Key here.

Flickr API Secret:

If you have a secret for the Flickr API, enter it here.

▷ Supported features

▷ ImageShack configuration

▷ Photobucket configuration

▷ Picasa configuration

Save configuration   **Reset to defaults**

Now add a new content type for **Photo Blog**. This content type will allow images to be posted from various providers, as supported by the module. After the type has been created, add a field for an **External Image**, selecting the **3rd Party Image** radio button. We'll name it **Provided Photo** for this example.

Under the **Providers Supported** fieldset, we'll leave all the boxes unchecked. If we wanted to exclude or include only certain providers, we would check the providers we wanted. Leaving them all unchecked will cause the module to allow all providers when embedding external images. This can be useful when new providers are added in the future, either by the module's maintainers or by your own custom code. So you don't need to reconfigure the field to add that support. On the other hand, you may have reasons to, for instance, only allow content from a certain provider:

At the time of this writing, you will also need to add your image sizes for three possible display sizes. Unfortunately, because the images are provided by an external server, there is no standard way to guarantee that the image will be retrieved at a certain size. There has been a discussion about fetching images and storing them on your server for use by other modules, such as **ImageCache**, but this has not yet been implemented.

For now, you can leave these settings alone, unless you wish to force your own size. When displayed, these images will be resized using HTML, which means the browser resizes rather than the server. This can cause image pixelation or distortion. Additionally, the module will attempt to find a reasonably close size when allowed by the provider, such as Flickr, to minimize distortion.

If you leave a width or height setting at 0, then the module will scale the photo with constant aspect ratio so that it is not distorted. Otherwise, the image will be forced to a certain size, for instance as a square thumbnail.

Three sizes are offered: Full size, Preview size, and Thumbnail. You will be familiar with this concept from earlier examples:

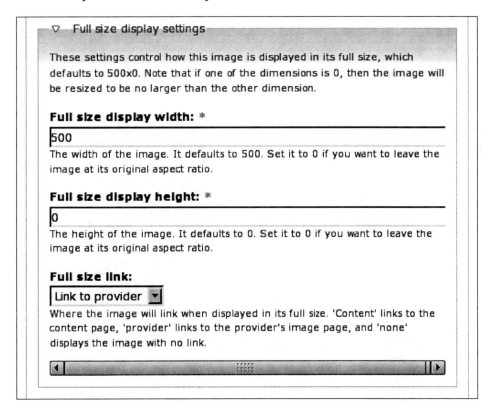

The link for each size may be set to **Link to provider**, which will link back to the original page from the provider, **Link to content**, which will link to the content node page, and **No link**, which will display the image with no link. For licensing purposes, most or all providers will require at least the full size image to link back to the original page. Check with the content provider if you have questions about this requirement:

Provided Photo:

http://flickr.com/photos/pingnews/291708133/

Enter the URL or Embed Code here. The embedded third party content will be parsed and displayed appropriately from this.

The following services are provided: Flickr, ImageShack, Photobucket, Picasa

Now add a new **Photo Blog** entry. You will see a new field asking for a URL or **Embed Code.** Simply copy and paste the URL from the original Flickr (or other provider's) page, enter a title, and submit your new content.

Embedded Media Field will automatically determine that the URL comes from Flickr and display the image properly:

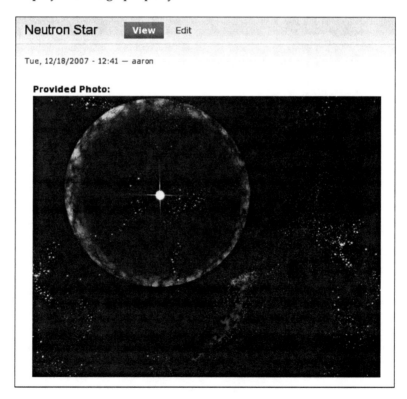

Views for Galleries and Slideshows

Even with all these features that extend image capability for Drupal, our sites want more. Fortunately, using the tools we have covered in the last two chapters, we now have a powerfully flexible set of options to create custom displays.

The Dead Presidents Glee Society has asked us to create a gallery and slideshow of their favorite US presidents. This job should be a snap now. We'll just create a content type with an image field, two views, and a new **ImageCache** preset. Rather than using an image field, we could just as easily use **Image Attach** with **Image** nodes.

We'll call this content type **President**, and create an **Image field** called **Image**. In many sites, it might be easiest to reuse existing **Image fields** among content types, saving you some work. In fact, you can even override many of the settings of these fields for specific content types such as the **Image path** or the **Maximum resolution**.

Now we'll create our view. Add a new view, and this time we'll set the page options. After setting your basic information, open the **Page** fieldset and check the **Provide Page View** box. Set its **URL** to presidents, the **View Type** to **List View**, and give it a **Title**. If you want the page to show up in your menu, then open the **Menu** subsection and check the **Provide Menu** box:

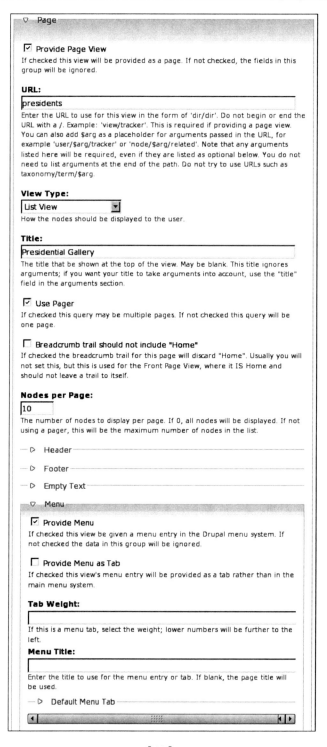

Under **Fields**, add **Node: Title**, and **Image: Image** (or whatever image field you've set for the type). For the image field's **Option**, select the **ImageCache** preset you want to use, which may be the fish_article_thumbnail from the previous example or another you've created.

The **Filters** will be **Node: Type** with a value of **President**, and (as almost always) **Node: Published**. Sort by **Node: Created Time (Descending)** and save your view.

After you add a few nodes, you'll have a basic gallery. Navigate to your new /presidents page to see the results. On a production site you'll certainly want to style the view differently, for instance by floating your images or at the very least replicating the styles of the **Image Gallery** module. No worries, we'll cover some techniques for doing this in the next chapter.

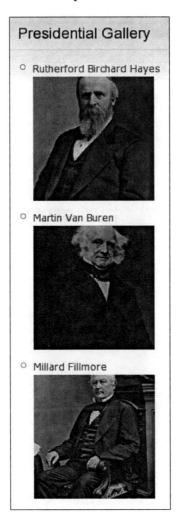

We'll also create a dynamic slideshow block for our gallery as well. Install the **Views Slideshow** module (available at `http://drupal.org/project/views_slideshow`). Then edit your new view by clicking on the **Edit** tab when viewing its page. Provide a **Block** view, select **Slideshow List** for the **View Type**, enter **10 Nodes per Block**, and check the **[More] Link** checkbox.

Now enable that block (from **Administer | Site building | Blocks** at `/admin/build/block`), and you will have a dynamic slideshow built with JQuery.

The **Views Slideshow** module has many options available to it, including controlling the fade speed, slideshow mode (including a display of thumbnails that may be hovered on to change the main image), and other options:

Slideshow mode:

○ Single frame
◉ Thumbnail hover

Hover breakout:

◉ Teaser
○ Full

Hover breakout determines how to display the breakout element of the *Thumbnail hover* mode, either as a teaser or full node. It is ignored in *Single frame* mode.

☒ Display teasers last
When the mode is thumbnail hover, this determines whether to print the teasers first or second.

Mouse hover:

◉ Hover

The HoverIntent module, if installed, adds the *HoverIntent* option here. Selecting it causes a delay when the mouse hovers, to stop quick flybys from triggering the behavior. Selecting *Hover* chooses the default mouse behavior.

Timer delay (in milliseconds):

```
5000
```

Slideshow sort order:

◉ Forward
○ Reverse
○ Random

This option determines the sort order of the returned results within the slideshow. Note that it is not related to the View's sorting options, and will only affect resulting items.

☒ Fade
If checked, then the slideshow will fade between frames. Otherwise, the Fade speed and value, below, will be ignored.

Fade speed:

◉ Slow
○ Normal
○ Fast

Fade value:

```
0.25
```

The opacity to fade to, between 0 (fully transparent) and 1 (fully opaque).

User Images

So far, we have covered the use of images with node content on a site. There are other places you might want images to appear such as when associated with **Users** and **Taxonomy**, for instance.

For users, at the most basic, you can provide a user avatar by going to **Administer | User management | User settings** (at /admin/user/settings):

Pictures

Picture support:

○ Disabled

◉ Enabled

Enable picture support.

Picture image path:

| pictures |

Subdirectory in the directory *files/* where pictures will be stored.

Default picture:

| |

URL of picture to display for users with no custom picture selected. Leave blank for none.

Picture maximum dimensions:

| 85x85 |

Maximum dimensions for pictures, in pixels.

Picture maximum file size:

| 30 |

Maximum file size for pictures, in kB.

Picture guidelines:

This text is displayed at the picture upload form in addition to the default guidelines. It's useful for helping or instructing your users.

This allows the users to upload images representing themselves by editing their user account page. This image will then be displayed on their user page and will be available when creating views, both for node listings and user listings (as **User: Picture** in **Fields**). Also, you may display user pictures in posts and comments by enabling those options at the Themes administration page (browse to **Administer | Site building | Themes | Configure** at /admin/build/themes/settings).

Taxonomy Images

The **Taxonomy Image** module (at http://drupal.org/project/taxonomy_image) is a suite of modules for associating and displaying images with taxonomy.

Our client, Big Topsy Turvy, is a blog watching big-name circus performers. They want a category view that lists blog posts matching various types of performers such as clowns, acrobats, ring masters, and so on.

We will use the standard taxonomy listing with an image displayed at the top associated with the taxonomy term. This will require creating a small custom module to work in conjunction with the **Taxonomy Image** module.

Due to the organic nature of Drupal, it's certainly possible that by the time this goes to press, the **Taxonomy Image** (or another) module will handle this functionality automatically. However, this is still a good overview of how to override a theme function with a module.

First install the **Taxonomy Image** module. You'll also need to configure permissions giving access to users to view the taxonomy images, and perhaps for editors to administer them.

Next, create a vocabulary for our circus performers. Make sure to associate it with at least one content type, and enter a few terms. After doing this, go to the **Taxonomy** administration page again and click on the **Images** tab (at /admin/content/ taxonomy/taxonomy_image).

Here you will see a list of all your terms, and you may upload a new image. Add a few images to associate with terms before continuing:

Name	Node Types	Image	Op
Circus Performers	page, image, blog, article		
Acrobats		*none*	edit term
Clowns			edit term
Lion Tamers		*none*	edit term

Now we're going to override the theme that displays taxonomy listings. We'll need to know which function to override. We can browse the Drupal API at `http://api.drupal.org/` to find this, searching for `theme_taxonomy` to see which functions come up.

The `theme_taxonomy_term_page` function sounds like the most likely candidate, from both its name and its description: **Render a taxonomy term page HTML output**.

> If we were uncertain, we could trace the code further, in this case by examining the code for the `taxonomy_menu` function to see what gets called. Here the `$items['taxonomy/term/%']` path calls `taxonomy_term_page`, which in turn calls our theme function via `theme('taxonomy_term_page')`. In the upcoming theming chapters, we'll learn alternative methods for tracing our theme functions using the **Theme developer** module.

This function is defined by default as the following:

```
function theme_taxonomy_term_page($tids, $result) {
  drupal_add_css(drupal_get_path('module', 'taxonomy') .'/taxonomy.
css');
  $output = '';
  // Only display the description if we have a single term, to avoid
clutter and confusion.
  if (count($tids) == 1) {
    $term = taxonomy_get_term($tids[0]);
    $description = $term->description;
    // Check that a description is set.
    if (!empty($description)) {
      $output .= '<div class="taxonomy-term-description">';
      $output .= filter_xss_admin($description);
      $output .= '</div>';
    }
  }
  $output .= taxonomy_render_nodes($result);
  return $output;
}
```

We only need to add `$output .= taxonomy_image_display($term->tid);` the description for the term in order to add our custom image, when provided. For this, we'll need to first create a new module to add our theme function override.

You will need to first create a folder in your `/sites/all/modules` directory, which we'll descriptively call `taxonomy_page_override`. Create two files called `taxonomy_page_override.info` and `taxonomy_page_override.module`.

Type the following into `taxonomy_page_override.info`, which will define our module. This will allow the module to be displayed on our module administration page. Place it in the **Taxonomy Image** package and make it dependent on the `taxonomy_image` module.

This dependency is required as we'll call the `taxonomy_image_display` function from our module, which is defined in the parent module. We would encounter runtime errors if we did not have the two modules working in tandem.

```
; $Id$
name = Taxonomy Page Override
description = Override our theme_taxonomy_page to add taxonomy images.
dependencies[] = taxonomy_image
core = 6.x
package = Taxonomy Image
```

Next, type the following into the taxonomy_page_override.module file, which will create our override function:

```php
<?php
// $Id$
/**
 *   Implement hook_theme_registry_alter.
 */
function taxonomy_page_override_theme_registry_alter(&$theme_registry)
{
  // Override the standard theme_taxonomy_term_page function callback.
  $theme_registry['taxonomy_term_page']['function'] = 'taxonomy_page_
override_taxonomy_term_page';
}
/**
 *    This is our custom override for theme_taxonomy_term_page.
 *  It will add an image to the top of our taxonomy term node
 *  listing pages. Note that we're not calling it a theme_ function,
 *  to avoid confusion in the future, as this is defined with
 *  a theme registry alteration, rather than as a standard theme
 *  function.
 */
function taxonomy_page_override_taxonomy_term_page($tids, $result) {
  drupal_add_css(drupal_get_path('module', 'taxonomy') .'/taxonomy.
css');
  $output = '';
  // Only display the description if we have a single term, to avoid
clutter and confusion.
  if (count($tids) == 1) {
    $term = taxonomy_get_term($tids[0]);
    $description = $term->description;
    // Here is our new line. It will display the image, if available.
    $output .= taxonomy_image_display($term->tid);
    // Check that a description is set.
    if (!empty($description)) {
      $output .= '<div class="taxonomy-term-description">';
      $output .= filter_xss_admin($description);
      $output .= '</div>';
    }
  }
  $output .= taxonomy_render_nodes($result);
  return $output;
}
```

Now, when you enable your custom module and browse to a taxonomy listing page, you will see the taxonomy term image displayed proudly at the top of the page.

You can test this by entering some content, making sure while submitting to select a taxonomy term that has an associated image. Then click on the taxonomy link for that node, which will bring you to `/taxonomy/term/[tid]`:

We all love clowns! Well, except for those unfortunate sufferers of Coulrophobia. The following content celebrates those ridiculous entertainers from the world over!

Always Clowning Around...

Wed, 07/30/2008 - 22:22 — aaron

Ut libero turpis, accumsan non, vestibulum ut, interdum a, augue! Nullam arcu turpis; euismod at, tempus quis, dapibus cursus; odio. Aenean sollicitudin, pede non fermentum semper, erat lacus scelerisque mauris, sit amet bibendum ipsum nulla ac sapien. Nullam fermentum dolor vel neque pulvinar fermentum. Duis erat! Donec nec sapien non tellus sagittis tincidunt. Duis convallis leo in velit. Phasellus eget augue. Nunc eleifend turpis sit amet nulla. Fusce pharetra ultrices sem. Sed nec est? Vivamus posuere diam eget nunc. Donec tempor leo quis erat. Nunc sit amet massa.

aaron's blog   Add new comment   Read more   **Clowns**

Clowns put out Fire!

Wed, 07/30/2008 - 22:22 — aaron

Nam vestibulum consectetuer leo? Cras at tellus eget erat mollis vulputate. Morbi sagittis condimentum purus. Aliquam at enim sit amet nibh accumsan ultricies. Etiam auctor. Integer mauris erat, viverra ac, vulputate a, scelerisque sit amet,

There are several other methods we could have used to override the theme function, including the more traditional PHPTemplate theme function override (which we'll practice in the next chapter), or even by enabling the default `taxonomy_term` view and adding a PHP call to the `taxonomy_image_display` in the view's header. However, in general, moving theme override functions to custom modules makes future upgrades and porting code to other sites easier.

Summary

This chapter has taken us deep into the world of developing sites that embrace images. We have learned not only to create our own node types that use image fields, but also views to display only the content we wish. We can now use **ImageCache** to scale and crop images before display. Slideshows and custom galleries are in our command, as are integrating images with user accounts and taxonomy categories.

In the next chapter, we'll explore theming images to customize our output.

4
Theming Images

You will, without doubt work with various themes of Drupal. Inevitably, you will want or need to create a site that doesn't look like it came out of the box. This requires that you jump into the theme. Every new installation begins with the **Garland** theme, but most themers will usually alter this theme, adopt another, or even create a new theme from scratch. The techniques we will study here are practiced on the **Garland** theme, but may be adapted to any theme, although some may require alterations. By the end of this chapter, you should have a firm threshold from where to begin your work.

You should already have a custom theme to work from, as outlined in the first chapter. We assume you have copied the **Garland** folder to something similar to `/sites/themes/my_theme`, have made the necessary changes to `garland.info` (both changing that file's name to `my_theme.info` and making similar changes within that file), and have activated that new theme by visiting **Administer | Site building | Themes**.

You may choose to work from a different base theme, or even from scratch. The techniques examined here may or may not work, but in most cases would probably require only a little modification to achieve the desired results.

Many themers prefer to work from the **Zen** theme. In many ways, this may be preferable because of the extensive documentation available for that theme, the strong community of themers working to continue improving it, and its inherent extensibility. We chose not to use that theme in this book as installing a new subtheme for Zen would have added an unnecessary level of complexity to our examples, and also because the **Garland** theme is installed by default. However, you are strongly encouraged to try that theme out to see if it may suit your needs. The theme is available at `http://drupal.org/project/zen`.

Styling a View

In the last chapter you probably noticed that although we controlled what content was the output, its display was often less than desirable. This did not escape the attention of our friends at the Dead Presidents Glee Society. They like their gallery, but would rather see the thumbnails of their Presidents ordered horizontally, rather than vertically, with nice boxes around each entry.

If you have the **Presidential Gallery** view created from the last chapter, then we'll begin modifying it. Otherwise, you should create either that content type and view, or a new content type with an image field (named **Image**), and a page view of the **List View** type displaying node titles and image fields.

Open (or create) the `style.css` file of your custom theme or subtheme for editing. At the bottom, enter the following CSS code:

```
.view-presidents .view-item-presidents {
  float: left;
  margin: 0 5px 5px;
  padding: 10px;
  background: #eee;
  border: 1px solid gray;
}
```

This will cause the presidential images to float horizontally across the page, with a border around each and a gray background. Next, we'll pad things out with the margin and padding.

To give a white matte to the photographs that will help them to stand out, we'll also add the following just below that:

```
.view-presidents img {
  background: white;
  border: 1px solid gray;
  padding: 3px;
}
```

Finally, in the **Garland** theme we need to override the padding normally applied to items in a list with the following:

```
.view-presidents ul li {
  padding: 0;
}
```

This gives us a result like the following. Additionally, as the classes will be the same for a page view or a block view, our styles will apply to both the **Presidential Gallery** page at /presidents, and to the slideshow block we created in the last chapter.

Investigating a Theme

There are times when we want to investigate how a theme is created from a live preview, rather than (or in conjunction with) examining the source code. Fortunately, there are several tools available for this task. We'll look at two good options:

- **Firebug** — for examining the styles applied to a page
- **Theme Developer** — a module that lays open the inner workings of a Drupal theme.

Firebug

Firebug is a plug-in extension for Firefox. A powerful and invaluable aid for themers, this allows us to inspect the applied stylesheet classes in any web page and to make live changes. This helps to remove the guesswork and speeds up the process of trial and error.

Available from `http://getfirebug.com`, the extension is easy to install and has many options such as viewing and editing the various CSS of a page, a JavaScript viewer and console, an HTML inspector, and more.

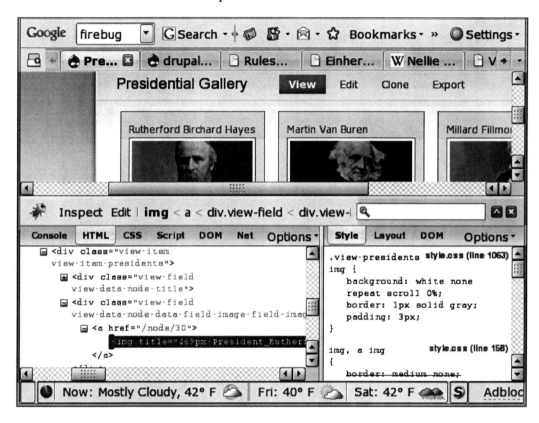

When adding stylesheet changes to views and other output from Drupal, you will often need to examine the final markup from a page to see how the classes and IDs are named. Firebug allows you to inspect the code as you view the page, even showing which styles are overridden by the descending stylesheets.

 Unfortunately, at this time there is nothing comparable to Firebug for Internet Explorer. But Microsoft does provide a moderately useful Developer Toolbar, available from its website.

Theme Developer Module

An exciting module released earlier this year is the Theme Developer module, which has been called the Firebug for Drupal. It is not available for Drupal versions earlier than 6. It will allow a themer to click on any section of the screen and expose the theme functions underlying the page content. The module is available at `http://drupal.org/project/devel`:

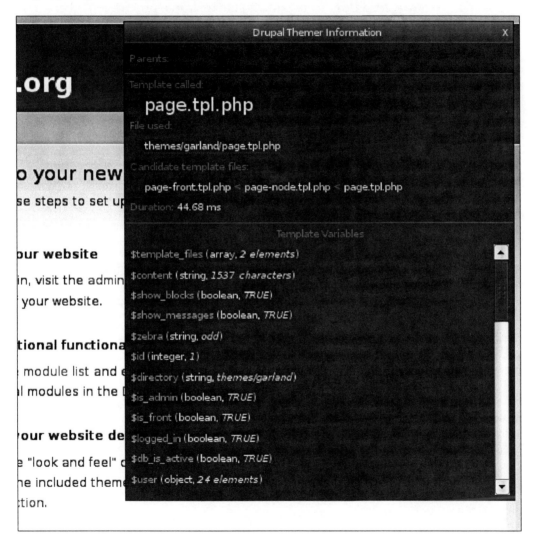

Overriding Image Nodes

Often, we need to re-theme a page or section of a page. Sometimes we can use existing classes and markup, and simply make changes to our stylesheet to accomplish this as with the previous examples. At other times, however, the markup is not exactly as we need it. So we need to override Drupal's output directly.

To this end, we can override any theme function that Drupal provides. But before we go into more detail, let's look again at nodes.

When nodes are displayed, **PHPTemplate** will output its content using specially named template files. Drupal will first look for a file named `node-TYPE.tpl.php` in the theme directory, where `TYPE` is the node's type. Failing to find this, it will use the theme's `node.tpl.php`. Finally, if that file doesn't exist as well then it will use the default `node.tpl.php` found in the **Node** module's directory (at `/modules/node/node.tpl.php`).

As an example, we'll quickly look at image nodes. Let's say that our editor doesn't want image attribution on the image node pages, but does want the submission date. We need to change the line that says something like **Wed, 01/02/2008 - 22:06 — aaron** to read **Wednesday, January 2, 2008** instead.

 If we didn't want the date as well, we could just visit Drupal's **Themes Global settings** page by browsing to **Administer | Site building | Themes** and selecting the **Configure** tab (at `/admin/build/themes/settings`), and uncheck **Display post information on Image**.

We'll copy the `node.tpl.php` in our theme directory to `node-image.tpl.php` and use it as a base. (If your theme doesn't have that file, you can always copy the file from `/modules/node`.)

We will take a quick peek through Firebug and see that this line is contained in a `<span>` tag with a submitted class. Looking at our `node-image.tpl.php`, (assuming we're working from **Garland** or the default **Node** module), we see that all we need to do in this case is modify the lines from our theme that read:

```
<?php if ($submitted): ?>
  <span class="submitted"><?php print $submitted ?></span>
<?php endif; ?>
```

The `$submitted` variable is what we want. To see what creates the data for that module, we'll turn on our Theme Developer module, check the **Themer info** box at the bottom left of the page, and click on the submitted date on the screen:

Tracing this, we see that **theme_node_submitted** is overridden by **phptemplate_node_submitted** (defined in our theme's **template.php** function), and would be further overridden by **mytheme_node_submitted** if that function existed.

We could be tempted to simply override that behavior by creating our own override at the template level. However, that would override the submitted info on all our node types, and we only want to do this for images.

So first we'll see how `$submitted` is built, as defined in our **template.php** file:

```
function phptemplate_node_submitted($node) {
  return t('!datetime — !username',
    array(
      '!username' => theme('username', $node),
      '!datetime' => format_date($node->created),
    ));
}
```

This would read something like **Wed, 01/02/2008 – 22:06 — aaron**.

Following the default behavior of **Garland**, we'll check to see if the `$submitted` variable exists, and then print an override for our images.

Replace the `if/endif` block for displaying the `$submitted` variable with the following code (where `l` in the `format_date` function is a lower-cased L):

```
<?php if ($submitted): ?>
  <span class="submitted"><?php print t('Image uploaded on !date.',
array('!date' => format_date($node->created, 'custom', 'l, F j, Y')));
?></span>
  <?php endif; ?>
```

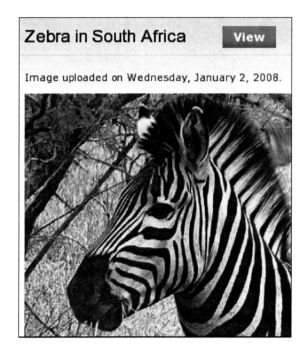

The `t()` function allows any text within to be translated. Obviously, this usually won't be necessary when overriding a theme function for a specific site, but it is a good practice in any case. That function will replace `!date` with our custom date, which is defined using the PHP formatting options found at `http://us.php.net/date`.

Image Effects

It is a common request to apply certain image effects to a page such as rollover menus and drop shadows. We'll take a look at how to do these, and more. There are plenty of so-called "eye-candy" modules, particularly those that implement jQuery, which will help to do other similar techniques. By examining how themes are created, it is possible to create new effects by building on what we learn here.

Rollover Menus

A common need with sites is to use graphical menus, sometimes with rollover images. We'll tackle both the needs here by creating a header menu using the following image named `primary-links.png`, which is 420-pixels wide and 80-pixels high and is placed into the theme's `/images` folder:

The top-half of the image is meant to be the menu as it appears on the screen, while each section of the bottom-half will be displayed when the mouse cursor rolls over a menu item.

First, let's take a quick look at how menus are created. In Drupal, we have three built-in menus with the ability to add more as desired. These are the Navigation menu, the Primary menu, and the Secondary menu.

Most familiar will be the Navigation menu — By default, this is displayed in the left sidebar, is titled with the **user's name,** and contains links to such items as the **user's account, log out, administration** (when allowed), and so on.

The primary menu in the **Garland** theme (and most others available from Drupal) will be displayed at the top header, while the Secondary menu will be displayed in the bottom footer. Both these menus are empty by default. But if you add items, they will appear in the relevant sections. Menus are output as blocks, so may be moved to other regions and otherwise controlled in the **Blocks** administration page.

The menu in this example will be the site's Primary menu that is displayed at the top of each page. Go to the **Menus** administration page (at **Administration | Site building | Menus**) and click on **Primary links**, which brings you to `/admin/build/menu-customize/primary-links`. (In Drupal 5, there isn't a link for **Primary links**, but the following will be the same.)

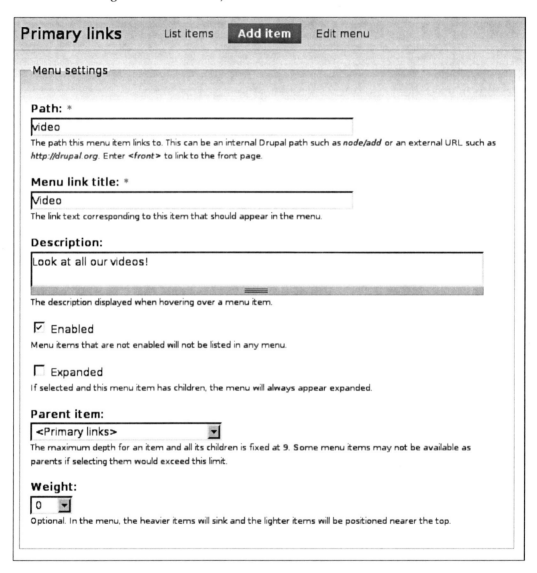

Now click on **Add item** (at /admin/build/menu-customize/primary-links/add, and in Drupal 5 at /admin/build/menu/item/add/2) and add some links to your Primary menu. In this case, it will be a link for **Home** (going to <front>), **Video** (going a view we created at /video), **Photo** (going to the **Image gallery** at /image), and **Links** (which links to a page node with our favorite links at node/11). On the **menu** administration page, after creating your links, you'll be able to change the order of the menu items by dragging their anchors, which otherwise appear in alphabetical order.

At the end of this, we'll have a menu at the top of the page:

If we examine the page source for this, we see something like the following:

```
<ul class="links primary-links"><li class="menu-23143 first">
                        <a href="/" title="Home Page">Home</a></li>
<li class="menu-23144"><a href="/image" title="Image gallery">Image
                                                        </a></li>
<li class="menu-23145"><a href="/video" title="Video gallery">Video
                                                        </a></li>
<li class="menu-23146 last"><a href="/node/11" title="About us">
                                                About us</a></li>

</ul>
```

Menus in Drupal are output as an item list, which allows us great flexibility in theming. The entire menu is an unordered list (<ul>) with two classes: links and the name of the menu, in this case primary-links.

Each list item (<li>) has a unique class for the menu item and the first and last items are further delineated. In Drupal 5, the unique list item classes will be different, but still unique per link. That's what's important here.

Slicing Images

To create the styles for our image rollovers, we're first going to place the top half of the image in the **Primary links** container. Then each link will be positioned appropriately, and the **hover** attribute will overlay the appropriate section of the bottom half of the image over that. The text of each link item will also be removed from the display, although it will still technically be present, allowing for menu accessibility when browsers may have images or CSS turned off.

Next we need to a little math. We have to find the position for each button in our image. Opening it in Gimp, Photoshop, or some other image manipulation program, we determine the following values for the top left corner of each section, as illustrated here:

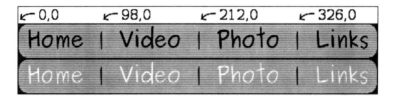

Thus as each half of the image is 40-pixels wide, our **Home** button will be the rectangle defined with the top-left margin of 0,0 and the bottom-right margin of 97,39. The section defined when hovering with a mouse will be at 0,40 and 97,79. The first number of each sequence is the X value (left to right), and the second is the Y value (top to bottom).

Cascading Style Sheets (CSS)

A large part of a themer's job is to understand and be able to modify the styles of a page. This is done by writing CSS.

Drupal heavily utilizes CSS to make pages appear and behave in a certain way. In fact, it is this behavior that helps drive an often heard criticism of all Drupal sites looking similar. This is a boon for some pages that "just work" when we plug in our modules, and a curse as it can often be difficult to override Drupal's base styles with other desired behaviors. We're going to touch briefly upon stylesheets here, but you are encouraged to seek other sources to learn CSS more deeply.

Now that we have the values for our image menu sections, we can begin writing the CSS for this menu. Enter the following code at the bottom of `style.css` to get things started:

```
ul.primary-links li a,
ul.primary-links li a:link,
ul.primary-links li a:visited {
   background: url(images/primary-links.png);
   display: block;
   height: 40px;
   margin: 0;
   padding: 0;
}
```

This will set each link to display the background image. They will be displayed as a block so that clicking anywhere in the area defined by the link will activate the link. The height will be 40px to display only the top half of the image. We also need to remove margins and padding from the links as well. Looking at the results, we also need to override the **Garland** theme's padding for primary link items with the following:

```
ul.primary-links li {
  padding: 0;
}
```

Now, we need to define the area for each link using the coordinates we determined earlier. (The widths are determined using simple arithmetic from our coordinates.) Note that the unique class assigned to a menu item may be different, depending on the menu's ID. It is also different in Drupal 5. The best way to determine the individual class names is to examine the page in Firebug or to examine the HTML source:

```
ul.primary-links li.menu-23143 a {
  width: 97px;
}
ul.primary-links li. menu-23144 a {
  background-position: -98px 0;
  width: 114px;
}
ul.primary-links li. menu-23145 a {
  background-position: -212px 0;
  width: 114px;
}
ul.primary-links li. menu-23146 a {
  background-position: -326px 0;
  width: 94px;
}
```

Each link now has a defined region. You should see the menu now displaying the top half of the image. By entering the following, you will see the bottom area of each link when hovering with the mouse:

```
ul.primary-links li. menu-23143 a:hover {
  background-position: 0 -40px;
}
ul.primary-links li. menu-23144 a:hover {
  background-position: -98px -40px;
}
ul.primary-links li. menu-23145 a:hover {
  background-position: -212px -40px;
}
ul.primary-links li. menu-23146 a:hover {
  background-position: -326px -40px;
}
```

Finally, we need to remove the text using an image replacement technique. We leave the text in the HTML for accessibility, but use our stylesheet to hide the text from browsers:

```
ul.primary-links {
   text-indent: -9000px;
}
```

There is more code required to make the list horizontal, but this is already present assuming you're using the **Garland** theme's `style.css` as a base. Other themes also do this. If you want to see more about styling menus, a good site to visit is `http://css.maxdesign.com.au/listamatic/`. For image replacement, a comprehensive start can be found at `http://www.mezzoblue.com/tests/revised-image-replacement/`.

Drop Shadows

Drop shadows around images are an often-requested feature. There are many methods that have been developed over time for doing this, from using CSS borders on the right and bottom to layered images to Flash to JavaScript.

Rather than delving too far into the possible techniques, we will apply the method described by Sergio Villarreal in *A List Apart*, shown at `http://www.alistapart.com/articles/cssdropshadows`.

This method involves wrapping an image with an extra div layer, applying CSS to give a background image of a shadow to the wrapper, and pulling the image to the left and up. Obviously, the CSS will be applied to `style.css`. To wrap our images in an extra div, however, we need to alter the appropriate `tpl` files.

For this exercise, we'll add drop shadows to images of the gallery thumbnails for the **Fish Article** nodes of the Fishtopian Society from the last chapter. (If you don't have that, then just make a quick node type with a multiple image field and follow along.) For good measure, we'll also change those thumbnails into links to a larger version of the image.

You'll first need to make a drop shadow image in your favorite image editor. This image needs to be large enough to cover the block area behind the image. You might make it slightly larger than the images if using **ImageCache**. Or for versatility and reusability, you might rather just make a large image, say 800x800 pixels. In Gimp, you would use the **Shadow** option in the **Script-Fu** menu after creating a blank white layer. In Photoshop, you'll use **Layer | Layer Style | Drop Shadow**. Other editors probably have similar methods to create drop shadows. Save the image as a PNG:

```
This image should be large enough
to encompass the largest expected images.

The top layer is just white.
The bottom layer is your drop shadow.

Note the width of the drop shadow.
In this case, it is 6 pixels.
```

For the sake of earlier versions of Internet Explorer, you'll also need to create a GIF version of the drop shadow with **transparency on,** using the same background color as the planned page background (white in our example).

If you want a copy of the drop shadow to work with, you can find some at the *A List Apart* tutorial or the versions used for this example at `http://drupalmultimedia. org/sites/drupalmultimedia.org/files/examples/drop-shadow.gif` and `http://drupalmultimedia.org/sites/drupalmultimedia.org/files/ examples/drop-shadow.png`.

We now need to put wrapper divs around our fish gallery images. To do this, we'll need to write a new `node-fish_article.tpl.php` file in our theme directory, copying `node.tpl.php` as earlier.

Examining that file, we see that the node's content is printed as follows:

```
<div class="content">
  <?php print $content ?>
</div>
```

Unfortunately, that doesn't really help us here. We need to find a way to grab our fields and print them directly, overriding the default content display.

Fortunately, **CCK** and **PHPTemplate** provide us handy variables for printing all the fields of a node. However, sometimes it can be difficult to determine what those might be.

One option, useful for other tasks such as debugging as well, is to print the entire node object. Type the following at the top of `node-fish_article.tpl.php`. Note that you do not want to do this on a live site:

```
<?php var_export($node); ?>
```

When you next look at a node of this type, at the top of the content area you will see a bunch of garbage; useful garbage, fortunately. It may start something like this:

```
stdClass::__set_state(array( ['nid'] => '22', ['vid'] => '22',
['type'] => 'fish_article', ['status'] => '1', ['created'] =>
'1197843638', ['changed'] => '1197844362', ['comment'] => '2',
['promote'] => '0', ['sticky'] => '0', ['revision_timestamp'] =>
'1197844362', ['title'] => 'Grouper', ['body'] =>
'Main Image: // etc ...
```

It can be difficult to ascertain what you're looking at from this display. You'll see a cleaner version in the page source:

```
stdClass::__set_state(array(
    ['nid'] => '22',
    ['vid'] => '22',
    ['type'] => 'fish_article',
    ['status'] => '1',
    ['created'] => '1197843638',
    ['changed'] => '1197844362',
    ['comment'] => '2',
    ['promote'] => '0',
    ['sticky'] => '0',
    ['revision_timestamp'] => '1197844362',
    ['title'] => 'Grouper',
    ['body'] => '<div class="field field-type-image field-field-main-
image"><div class="field-label">Main Image: </div> // etc ...
```

This begins with `stdClass::__set_state`, which is how our node is stored in memory. Each property of that array object is printed in its own line such as `['nid'] => '22'` or `['revision_timestamp'] => '1197844362'`. In your page source, you might actually see `=&gt;`, which is HTML markup for `=>`.

We'll scroll down until we see the property for our gallery fields. This will look something like the following:

```
['field_gallery_images'] => Array
        (
            ['0'] => Array
                (
                    ['fid'] => '148',
                    ['title'] => '800px-Gordon_-_Goliath_grouper.jpg',
                    ['alt'] => '800px-Gordon_-_Goliath_grouper.jpg',
                    ['nid'] => '22',
                    ['filename'] => '800px-Gordon_-_Goliath_grouper.
jpg',
                    ['filepath'] => 'sites/drupalmultimedia.org/files/
gallery_images/800px-Gordon_-_Goliath_grouper.jpg',
                    ['filemime'] => 'image/jpeg',
```

```
                    ['filesize'] => '73182',
                    ['view'] => '<img src="http://drupalmultimedia.
org/sites/drupalmultimedia.org/files/imagecache/fish_article_
thumbnail/files.dm/gallery_images/800px-Gordon_-_Goliath_grouper.
jpg" alt="800px-Gordon_-_Goliath_grouper.jpg" title="800px-Gordon_-
_Goliath_grouper.jpg">',
                    )
            ['1'] => Array
                (
                    ['fid'] => '149',
                    ['title'] => '793px-Blue-spotted.grouper.arp.jpg',
// etc...
```

There are two things we want from that: the field name `field_gallery_images` and the `view` property.

> It is in fact easier in most cases to install the **Devel** module, and use the resulting **Dev load** tab that appears on every node for administrators to retrieve the same information. There are some cases, however, in which you may want to directly print a variable. Using `var_export`, as opposed to `print_r` or the **Dev load** tab, will present a variable in a format that may often be pasted into PHP with fewer modifications to be made afterwards.

When we display our content, we'll need to print everything manually. That means we'll need to know all the fields to print. Quickly scanning the debugging output, we can determine all the fields to print. They will, helpfully, also correspond to the admin view at **Administer | Content management | Content types | Fish Article | Manage fields** (at `/admin/content/node-type/fish-article/fields`):

Fish Article	Edit	**Manage fields**	Display fields	Add field

Gallery Images   Main Image

Control the order of fields in the input form.

To change the order of a field, grab a drag-and-drop handle under the Label column and drag the field to a new location in the list. (Grab a handle by clicking and holding the mouse while hovering over a handle icon.) Remember that your changes will not be saved until you click the Save button at the bottom of the page.

Label	Name	Type	Operations	
⊹ Title				
⊹ Body				
⊹ Main Image	field_main_image	image	Configure	Remove
⊹ Gallery Images	field_gallery_images	image	Configure	Remove
⊹ File attachments				

Thus, the fields we need are **field_main_image** and **field_gallery_images**. We'll also need to deal with the `body`, which we'll get to in a moment. The `title` is not a part of the node's content in the template file as it is displayed separately. So we don't need to worry about that.

Each of the image fields will have the same type of array. The main image array will only have one value, an array keyed to `field_main_image[0]`. We could print `$node->field_main_image[0]['view']`, but because overriding node content is a common need, the PHPTemplate developers have added all node fields as variables available to themers. Thus, we'll only need to print `$field_main_image[0]['view']`.

This will be printed before the content body. So let's add this quickly, replacing the `<?php print $content ?>` line (and removing our debugging statement of `<?php var_export($node); ?>`):

```
<?php print $field_main_image[0]['view']; ?>
```

If you examine the node now, you will only see the main image with no other content. If there is no main image, you will see no content at all.

Next we need the body. It might be tempting to just print `$node->body`, but this will just display the entire node content as with the original `$content`. Even though our content description is stored in the `$node->body` property, any other fields of the node are merged into that before the node is passed on to our theme.

The original body is stored at `$node->content['body']['#value']` with just the text we want now. We'll be able to print this right after the main image.

The gallery images consist of an unknown number of arrays beginning with 0. So if we have three images, they'll be keyed to `field_gallery_images[0]`, `field_gallery_images[1]`, and `field_gallery_images[2]`.

Because of this, we'll need to use a little code to loop through each field properly. That is the field we'll wrap with a new div. Putting it all together we'll now have this, which will replace the original `print $content`:

```php
<?php
  print $field_main_image[0]['view'] . "\n";
  print $node->content['body']['#value'] . "\n";
  foreach ($field_gallery_images as $image) {
    print "<div class='drop-shadow'>{$image['view']}</div>\n";
  }
?>
```

Of interest here is the `{$image['view']}`. We could have written that line as something like `print '<div class="drop-shadow">' . $image['view'] . "</div>\n"`, but using double quotes or "magic quotes" in PHP allows us to parse variables directly in the string. The curly `{}` brackets are only necessary because we're printing an array. A valid example of embedding a variable in a string would be `print "<div class='title'>$title</div>"`. The `\n` prints a new line that is only a white space in HTML, but makes the source a little easier to read.

We're almost there. If we examine a node page, we'll see the content we saw before we broke it up into its constituent fields. The only part left now is to add the required CSS for our drop shadows at the end of `style.css`:

```css
.drop-shadow {
  float:left;
  background: url(drop-shadow.png) no-repeat bottom right !important;
  background: url(drop-shadow.gif) no-repeat bottom right;
  margin-left: 10px !important;
  margin-left: 5px;
}
.drop-shadow img {
  display: block;
  position: relative;
  background-color: #fff;
  border: 1px solid #ccc;
  margin: -6px 6px 6px -6px;
  padding: 2px;
}
```

This will display the shadow as a background, beginning from its bottom right, and move the image up and left. The border and padding around the image will also create a frame and matte effect.

Unfortunately, you may have noticed that the node links such as to **add comments** are now to the right of the image galleries. This is because our images are floating. We need to fix that so the following links' div clears those floats. We'll need to change the content class statement adding the **clear-block** class to it:

```html
<div class="content clear-block">
```

You may also consider using a stronger fix than a simple clearfix, which may not be effective in older browsers. One of the most comprehensive fixes available is known as the **clearfix** class. See `http://www.positioniseverything.net/easyclearing.html` for more information on using this.

We also want to turn our images into links. On one hand, you could change the field settings to display the images as links by browsing to **Administer | Content management | Content types | Fish Article | Display fields,** at `admin/content/node-type/fish-article/display`. However, this would cause them to link back to the main node, whereas we want them to link to the larger images. This simply requires changing the code we wrote in `node-fish-article.tpl.php` to wrap our images in links:

```php
<?php
  print $field_main_image[0]['view'] . "\n";
  print $node->content['body']['#value'] . "\n";
  foreach ($field_gallery_images as $image) {
    $img = "<div class='drop-shadow'>{$image['view']}</div>";
    print l($img, $image['filepath'], array('html' => TRUE));
  }
?>
```

 The `array('html' => TRUE)` in the function (which prints a link) tells Drupal that the link is to be displayed as HTML, which is needed for an image link. In Drupal 5, you would use `print l($img, $image['filepath'], array(), NULL, NULL, FALSE, TRUE)` instead.

LightBox

A light box is an image that will pop up when a thumbnail is clicked on or hovered over. This will often gray out the underlying page. There are several modules providing this functionality for Drupal. As in many other instances, it can be difficult to determine the best light box module for your needs. There is a comparison of most of the available light box modules at `http://drupal.org/node/266126`.

For this chapter, we'll examine the **Lightbox 2** module available at `http://drupal.org/project/lightbox2`. In a later chapter we'll also look at the **Thickbox** module, which is supported by default with the **Embedded Media Field** module.

Once the **Lightbox 2** module is enabled, image node images will automatically have a light box on click. Adding it to other images such as **imagefield**s is fairly easy as well, and only requires adding a theme call to your `tpl` files.

We'll add that to our example as follows. Adding a `'rel'` tag of `'lightbox'` will turn the image into a lightbox link to the larger image. We can further group images by making that tag `'lightbox[fish-group]'`, so the images may be viewed with next/previous arrows:

```php
<?php
  print l($img, $image['filepath'], array('html' => TRUE, 'attributes'
=> array('rel' => 'lightbox[fish-group]')));
?>
```

 In Drupal 5, that would be `print l($img, $image['filepath'], array('rel' => 'lightbox[fish-group]'), NULL, NULL, FALSE, TRUE)`.

More Eye Candy

There are many other modules involving images that are worth exploring. Sadly, we can't examine them all here in detail due to a lack of space. However, here's a list to get you started.

Magnification

There are several options for image magnification or zoom. The **Magnifier** module available at `http://drupal.org/project/magnifier`, utilizing a jQuery plug-in of the same name, allows for image zooming. Likewise, the **Zoomify** module at `http://drupal.org/project/zoomify` provides the same functionality, albeit with a Flash application:

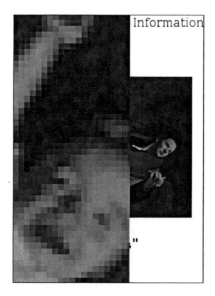

Star Ratings

Hands down, the most comprehensive solution for Drupal ratings is the **Five Star** module. It allows users to rate content and comments using a graphical interface. The module is simple to set up and customize:

Curabitur odio leo, ver
ac mi. Proin ac lorem v
Maecenas fermentum

Your rating:
★ ★ ★ ★ ☆

Watermarks

Watermarking is a technique of superimposing an image such as a logo over another image, usually with some transparency. The **Image watermark** module works in conjunction with the **Image** module to bring this to Drupal.

Slideshows

Image slideshows are frequently desired on a site. There are several modules for this functionality. For instance, the **Lightbox 2** module examined earlier handles slideshows specifically for images. However, other modules such as **jCarousel** and **Views Slideshow** allow any content to be viewable in a slideshow.

jCarousel is a jQuery slide show, suitable for images or any content that can be created in a list form. The original plug-in was written by Jan Sorgalla. Its default slide show is professional and works right out of the box, and new skins can be easily themed by creating new style sheets. It can work with any view, so you could use it to create an image slide show, a video slide show, a slide show of text, or any combination you could come up with.

After enabling the module, available at `http://drupal.org/project/jcarousel`, you would simply create a list view as desired, with the fields you need, and add the following code to the view header, with a PHP filter, replacing view-name with the CSS name of the view (such as view-jcarousel or view-favorite-photos). You can read the documentation for jCarousel options at `http://sorgalla.com/projects/jcarousel/`. The options for customization available are extensive, including auto scrolling, dynamic data callbacks, and custom animation effects.

```php
<?php
// Add the necessary CSS and js files to our view.
jcarousel_add();
// Create an initialization script.
$js = '$(document).ready(function() {
  // Transform our view into a jCarousel slideshow.
  var slideshow = $("div.view-name .view-content ul");
  slideshow.addClass("jcarousel-skin-tango");
  slideshow.jcarousel({
    scroll: 1
  });
});';
// Add the above jCarousel javascript.
drupal_add_js($js, 'inline');
?>
```

Summary

By the end of this chapter, you will have learned all the essentials of theming images in Drupal. We have covered overriding styles, image nodes, and image fields. We have learned how to call theme functions, and how to uncover hidden theme functions to wrap our images with. We have studied techniques and modules to create eye candy and add new functionality to our images such as drop shadows, light boxes, and slide shows. When we combine this with the information we learned in the prior image chapters, we have a strong foundation with which to create powerful, custom, image-rich sites.

In the following three chapters, we will add video to our repertoire. We will begin with Administering Video.

5

Third-Party Video

When adding video to a site, an administrator will first have to answer a basic question that will determine the direction to take when setting up the site: Will the site host its own videos or will it use a third party to host videos?

Only a few scant years ago, video on all but the largest sites was nearly unheard of due to bandwidth limitations and the dearth of available technology. However in a couple of years, adding video became more accessible, but was fairly difficult. But YouTube and providers of it transformed the Internet, allowing videos to be uploaded and embedded even within individual blog posts.

We now have many video options available, so the only question is which route to go. Hosting video can still be a prohibitive option, particularly if your site already expects a lot of bandwidth. Additionally, one may enjoy more exposure by using a third-party provider, although it does mean adding the branding of that provider, and sometimes their ads.

The benefit of hosting video is adding your own branding and possibly having this advertising space available, although some providers such as Revver have an ad revenue sharing option. YouTube has been hinting for some time that it will also allow revenue sharing. But at the time of this writing, that is not a reality. On the other hand, there may be copyright issues involved for which you should examine the relevant terms of service before making a decision.

Third-Party Video Providers

Many sites desiring video will choose to use a third-party video provider such as YouTube or Blip.TV. This reduces the bandwidth requirement from their server, is easy to include in their posts, and allows videos to be easily shared virtually by users across the Internet.

The easiest way, without further configuration of a basic Drupal installation, for an administrator to include a third-party video is to simply paste the video's embedded code in a post. Most video providers will offer a snippet of HTML that may be copied from a particular video page, which will embed the video.

However, this requires using a filter that will allow `<object>`, `<embed>`, and `<param>` tags. But since they open the door to attacks on the site, they should only be used by administrators and trusted editors. You could also use the **Full HTML** filter, but this is even more dangerous as allowing that filter to be generally used would open the site to **cross-site scripting (XSS)** attacks.

First, you'll need to set up a filter that allows the tags. Add an input format at **Administer | Site configuration | Input formats** (at `/admin/settings/filters/add`). After naming the filter, check the role(s) you wish to give access to this filter such as **edit role**. Check **HTML corrector**, **HTML filter**, and **Line break converter**. After pressing **Save configuration**, click on the **Configure** tab.

Using YouTube as an example, an administrator would first need to upload a video to YouTube. This will require an account at YouTube, but they make it fairly painless for a user to jump in and contribute videos. You'll just need to follow their instructions:

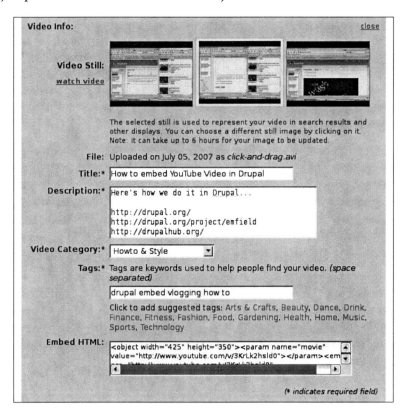

Once you have a video there, you will find the embedded code on the video page. You will need to click in the text field where that is provided, and copy the HTML for pasting on your own page:

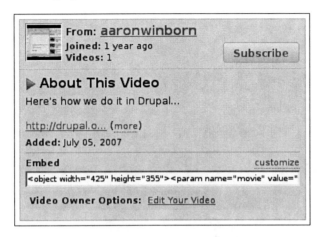

Next you will submit a node on your site such as from **Node | Add | Page** (at `/node/add/page`), and paste the embed code in the body for the node. You will need to enable either the new filter created earlier or **Full HTML**, as the embedded code will contain object and/or embedded tags, which would be filtered out by the default filter in Drupal.

 If you want editors to have the ability to select their filter, you will need to enable that ability for a role, and possibly set up a new filter depending on your needs. Also note that you will need to disable the TinyMCE Rich Text Editor when embedding video directly into content if the TinyMCE module is enabled on your site.

After submitting, your video will appear in the content. As with any HTML embedded in your node body, you may manually place your video at any point within the content such as after the second paragraph or at the end of the node:

Embedded Media Field

Finally, we come to the alternative of hosting video from our own servers. Although using a module such as **Media Mover** combined with services such as Amazon S3 makes serving video a slightly easier task than it might have otherwise been, for most sites the bandwidth required for serving video is generally not a viable option. Additionally, sites may wish to take advantage of the viral opportunities of hosting video through a widely recognized provider such as YouTube or Blip.TV.

There are several modules that provide some limited support for embedding third-party media, including both the **Video** and **Asset** modules. However, at the time of this writing, the most comprehensive and by far the easiest to configure and use is the **Embedded Media Field**, which includes the **Embedded Video Field** as part of its package.

Install both of these modules and set up a new content type with an Embedded Video Field. You will need, of course, to have the **CCK** (Content) module installed as well. As with our other examples, you will first add your type from **Administer | Content management | Content types | Add content type** (at /admin/content/types/add), give it a name such as Video, and add the field from **Administer | Content management | Content types | Video | Add field** (at /admin/content/node-type/video/add_field).

Before continuing, I must confess a bias here. I wrote the original **Embedded Media Field** module with assistance from Sam Tresler during DrupalCamp NYC in 2007, and rewrote it for a more solid and flexible API during OSCMS later that year. I am also indebted to Alex Urevick-Ackelsberg for his assistance in the ongoing maintenance and support.

```
Embedded Video
    ( 3rd Party Video
```

Without doing anything else, you may now add a new video from a provider by simply pasting its URL into the field. The module will then automatically parse and display the video appropriately.

There are several settings on the following page that may be set, including allowed providers, video and thumbnail sizes, and whether the video plays automatically.

You may leave the providers alone to allow content from any of them, or select only the providers you wish to allow editors and users to use:

▽ Providers Supported

Select which third party providers you wish to allow for this content type from the list below. If no checkboxes are checked, then all providers will be supported. When a user submits new content, the URL they enter will be matched to the provider, assuming that provider is allowed here.

Providers:

☐ Local

☐ Archive.org

☐ Blip.tv

☐ Brightcove

☐ Current TV

☐ Google

☐ iFilm

☐ JumpCut

☐ Live Video

☐ MetaCafe

☐ MySpace

☐ Revver

☐ Sevenload

☐ YouTube

☐ Custom URL

The local checkbox is experimental at the time of this writing and may not actually be on the version you're reading. The module maintainers (myself included, of course) intend to hook into other APIs to provide better local video support without reinventing the wheel. That may or may not be ready by the time you read this book.

The **Custom URL** provider is also used to experimentally support direct videos from any source available from an HTTP request, including your local server. It is not recommended for general use, as it would be easy to use that to unethically hotlink to videos from someone else's server. Hundreds of flying monkeys will hunt you down if you do that. Basically, always turn off support for that unless you have a specific (and moral) use for that feature.

You can set video sizes in the next sections for full size and preview size video display. By default, videos will be displayed in full size. You can change the display to video preview or thumbnail at the display settings page, by browsing to **Administer | Content management | Content types | Video | Display fields** (at `/admin/content/node-type/video/display`).

Videos will be forced to display at the size provided here, regardless of how they are offered by the provider. You can also determine if the video will autoplay or not. For instance, you might use a small video preview for teasers and a larger full-size video when viewing the node page, turning on the autoplay in that case:

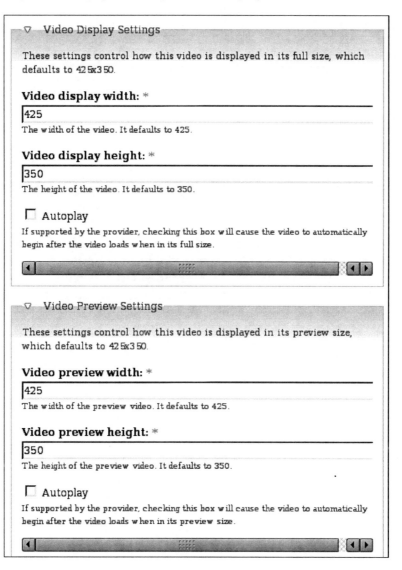

Finally, you may wish to use thumbnails, for instance when displaying a video as a teaser or when using views. Note that thumbnails are not yet supported for all video providers. Some providers do not offer an easy API to discover a particular video's thumbnail file:

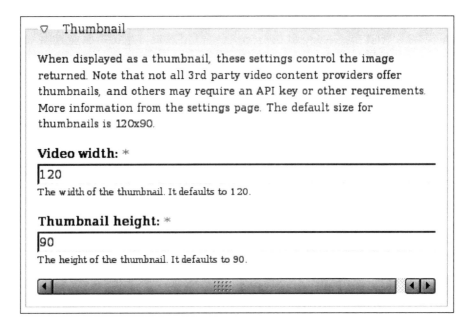

To learn if thumbnails are supported by a particular provider, go to **Administer | Content management | Embedded Media Field Configuration** (at /admin/ content/emfield) and open the fieldset for **Embedded Video Field**. You will see the supported features for each provider within their particular fieldsets, where you may also disable them or enable unique settings:

▽ YouTube configuration

These settings specifically affect videos displayed from YouTube. You can learn more about its API here.

☑ Allow content from *YouTube*

If checked, then content types may be created that allow content to be provided by *YouTube*.

☐ Show related videos

If checked, then when playing a video from YouTube, users may hover over the video to see thumbnails & links to related videos.

▷ YouTube API

▷ Embedded Video Player Colors

▽ Supported features

This is a list of the current state of support for the following features by *YouTube*:

Feature	Supported	Notes
Autoplay	Yes	
RSS Attachment	Yes	
Show related videos	Yes	This is embedded in the video itself when enabled; currently not available with other providers. Set the feature above.
Thumbnails	Yes	
Custom player colors	Yes	You may customize the player's skin by choosing your own colors, and/or border in that setting field set.

You may wish to provide for custom thumbnails, whether for providers lacking an automatic thumbnail or for any external video in general. For this purpose, the **Embedded Media Thumbnail** module is included in the module's package. Just enable that module, and then check the **Allow custom thumbnails for this field** box on the type's administration screen:

▽   Embedded Custom Thumbnails

☑ Allow custom thumbnails for this field

If checked, then editors may specify a custom thumbnail to be used, overriding any automatic thumbnails otherwise created.

Custom thumbnail label:

| emvideo custom thumbnail |

This label will be displayed when uploading a custom thumbnail.

Custom thumbnail description:

| If you upload a custom thumbnail, then this will be displayed when the |

This description will be displayed when uploading a custom thumbnail.

Maximum resolution for Images:

| 0 |

The maximum allowed custom thumbnail size expressed as WIDTHxHEIGHT (e.g. 640x480). Set to 0 for no restriction.

Image path:

| |

Optional subdirectory within the *"files.dm"* directory where images will be stored. Do not include trailing slash.

☐ Enable custom alternate text

Enable custom alternate text for custom thumbnails. Filename will be used if not checked.

☐ Enable custom title text

Enable custom title text for custom thumbnails. Filename will be used if not checked.

We now have a full-featured video field in place, which is as easy to use as cut and paste:

Submit emvideo

Title: *

YouTube Test

emvideo:

http://youtube.com/watch?v=3KrLk2hsld0

Enter the URL or Embed Code here. The embedded third party content will be parsed and displayed appropriately from this.

The following services are provided: Local, Archive.org, Blip.tv, Brightcove, Current TV, Dailymotion, GoLeft TV, Google, , JumpCut, Live Video, MetaCafe, MySpace, Revver, Sevenload, Tudou, YouTube, Custom URL

▽ emvideo custom thumbnail

| | Browse... |

If you upload a custom thumbnail, then this will be displayed when the emvideo thumbnail is called for, overriding any automatic thumbnails by custom providers.

Upload

Summary

Video is still a maturing media on the Internet. Much has happened as it has exploded onto sites across the world, and contributors to Drupal have made recent strides in supporting it. However, there is still much to be done to make it easier for administrators to support it. Also, although there are many new and traditional tools available such as Views and Embedded Media Field, these still require some set up to get working.

In the following chapters, we will examine how a developer may use Views and other tools to make embedding video easier for editors than it already is. We'll also see how to serve and brand videos from our local server.

6
Local Video

The past year has seen a major growth in videos on the Internet, and developers for Drupal have only recently really begun harnessing it. Several excellent modules have risen to the task, and their developers are working together to create strong offerings, increasingly working together to build an extensive and robust media API.

The **Video** module, holding a popular namespace, was an early contender for a one-stop solution. However, it has not been maintained well over the past year, leaving a gap in the offerings. Meanwhile, several alternatives have arisen in the past year and we will examine some of them.

There are basically two approaches for displaying video on your site: serving video from your own server, or embedding video from a third-party host. The last chapter examined remote videos, and this chapter will explore serving videos from your own server.

Local Video Files

When serving local video files, we have to consider first how a video will be placed onto the server and if we require any manipulation of the video. We may wish to use an upload field from a web form, or we may wish to use FTP to upload large files, or we may wish to be able to email a video to the server as from a cell phone. All of these options are available, so we will examine each in turn.

FileField

The first heavy hitter is the **FileField** module. This light-weight module goes a long way. At its most basic level, it adds the functionality of the core `Upload` module to CCK. Besides serving as an invisible API for `ImageField`, it can also expose file uploads as fields. The module supports any file type such as `.txt`, `.pdf`, images, video, or audio.

Before continuing, if you haven't already, you'll need to install the **FileField** module by downloading and enabling it from `http://drupal.org/project/filefield`.

Now we'll create a new content type called **Cartoon**. You'll need to add an `ImageField` to the node type, called `Cartoon Thumbnail`.

Next, set up a `FileField` also named **Cartoon**. For this example, our movies will always be **quicktime** files with a **mov** extension, since that's how our video editors will deliver their content.

Go to **Administer | Content management | Content types | Cartoon | Add field** (at `/admin/content/node-type/cartoon/add_field`). Enter the **Field name** of **Cartoon** and label of **Cartoon**, set the **Field type** to **File**, and click **Continue**. Leave the **Widget type** to **File Upload**, and press **Continue** again:

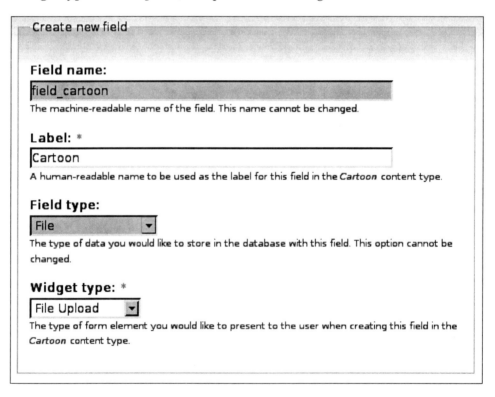

On the resulting screen, change **txt** in the **Permitted upload file extensions text field** to read `.mov` (without a "`.`" in front). In the **Global settings** fieldset, set the **Default list value** to **Listed** and **How should the file be listed?** to **Enforce default**. This will ensure the file is always listed with the node display:

Default list value: *

◉ Listed

○ Hidden

The list option determines whether files are visible on node views. This will be used as the default value for the list option.

How should the list value be handled?: *

○ User Configurable. (Users will be able to set the list value per file.)

◉ Enforce Default. (The default list value will be used for all files, and the list checkbox will not be displayed to users.)

Now add a video with its thumbnail from the content submission screen at **Create content | Cartoon** (at `/node/add/cartoon`). You'll see on the **Cartoon** field that it only allows `.mov` files; other file types will give a validation error.

You may not be able to add files above a certain size, depending on the PHP settings of your server. If you have the **Upload** module enabled, you can see your current upload size limit settings at **Administer | Site configuration | File uploads** (at `/admin/settings/uploads`). If you see something like **Your PHP settings limit the maximum file size per upload to 4 MB**, but you need to be able to upload 8 MB videos, you'll need to edit your `php.ini` file and add, for instance, `post_max_size = 8000000` and `upload_max_filesize = 8000000`.

Cartoon:

🎞 Sample.mov

54.32 KB

video/quicktime

Description:

Wallah Wallah

Replace:

[   ] Browse...

Maximum Filesize: *2 MB*

Allowed Extensions: *mov*

[Upload]   [Remove]

When you save this video node, you'll see a link to the video. Users could now click on that link to load the video in an external viewer. But that's obviously not what we have in our mind. We need to do a little more to make the video display in the browser:

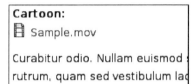

The `FileField` module is little more than an API for file handling. As `ImageField` does, other modules may tap into its functionality, allowing them all to be light-weight, flexible, and powerful.

Theme Your Video

When using the `FileField` module to display cartoons, we want to actually display our video, rather than just a listing of the video.

To make the `FileField` module work for our purposes, we'll need to add our own theme files. To spice things up, our client wants us to display a custom thumbnail before displaying the uploaded video after clicking the image. Additionally, they want a logo watermarked on the video while it plays.

We'll use a combination of `ImageField` and `FileField` for the first task. Set up the `ImageField` named `Cartoon Thumbnail`, configuring two **ImageCache presets**: `cartoon_thumbnail` and `cartoon_overlay`, which **Scale and Crop** to 100x100 and 240x360 respectively. If you are unfamiliar with the process of creating **ImageCache presets**, you can follow the instructions from the Developing for Images chapter for a refresher.

As of this writing, to use the `FileField` module to display your video, you need to add a theme function. This may have changed by the time you read this chapter; work is in progress to add better video support to that module. It may be that there is an option in the **Display fields** page for our **Cartoon** field at **Administer | Content management | Content types | Cartoon | Display fields** (at `/admin/content/types/cartoon/display`).

However, because we plan to override this with our overlay thumbnail, we're going to do this manually. This is a good exercise in overriding theme functions.

Preprocess Hook

We've already seen how to override a theme function by creating a
`phptemplate_[theme_name]` function. We've also seen how to override or create
a template file for a theme function with something like `[theme_name].tpl.php`.
There are times, however, when we want to do a bit of both. For instance, we may
wish to make new variables available to a template file, and keep the PHP largely
separate from the HTML.

We can achieve this by tapping into the theming structure with a preprocess hook.
Specifically, we can create a `preprocess_[theme_name]` function to add variables
that would then be available to `[theme_name].tpl.php`.

We're going to take advantage of this to override the default `filefield` link.

 For more information about preprocess hooks than what we're about to
cover, visit `http://drupal.org/node/223430`.

Examining the `theme_filefield_file` function, we see the following code of
the alpha version of the module available at this time (in `/sites/all/modules/`
`filefield/filefield_formatter.inc`):

```
/**
 * Theme function for the 'generic' single file formatter.
 */
function theme_filefield_file($file) {
  $path = $file['filepath'];
  $url = file_create_url($path);
  $icon = theme('filefield_icon', $file);
  return '<div class="filefield-file clear-block">'. $icon .
l($file['filename'], $url) .'</div>';
}
```

We want to override this to display an embedded object for a movie file. We could
simply overwrite the function by creating a `phptemplate_filefield_file` or
`my_theme_filefield_file` function. But we also wish to create a template file
available for our themer who may wish to insert specific style classes or wrappers,
and we want that file to be easily maintainable in the future.

Therefore, we'll use this theme as a base, and additionally create a `$object` variable
that will contain our movie object, while leaving links in place for other types of files.

Let's first create our template file named `filefield_file.tpl.php` in our theme directory with the following code:

```php
<?php
/**
 *  filefield_file.tpl.php
 *  This will display the file object or link for all filefields.
 *  The following variables are available:
 *    $file: The original file object.
 *    $url: The URL to the file itself.
 *    $icon: A representative icon based on the file's mime type.
 *    $object: The HTML to display our file, as an object or link.
 */
?>
<div class="filefield-file clear-block">
  <?php print $object; ?>
</div>
```

As we see here, we're making more variables available to the template file than we plan to use. This makes future changes easier, particularly when we document this.

Now in `template.php`, add the following function. Note that any item inserted into the `$variables` array will be made available to our template file as a variable with the name of its key. So `$variables['object']` will later become `$object`:

```php
/**
 *  implement hook_preprocess_filefield_file.
 *  This interjects itself in the theme('filefield_file')
 *  structure, creating variables available for use by
 *  fielfield_file.tpl.php.
 */
function phptemplate_preprocess_filefield_file(&$variables) {
  $file = $variables['file'];
  $path = $file['filepath'];
  $url = file_create_url($path);
  $variables['url'] = $url;
  $variables['icon'] = theme('filefield_icon', $file);
  if ($file['filemime'] == 'video/quicktime') {
    $variables['object'] = <<<OBJECT
<object classid="clsid:02BF25D5-8C17-4B23-BC80-D3488ABDDC6B"
  codebase="http://www.apple.com/qtactivex/qtplugin.cab"
  width="360" height="240">
  <param name="src"
    value="$url" />
  <param name="controller" value="true" />
```

```
            <param name="autoplay" value="true" />
            <!--[if !IE]>-->
            <object type="video/quicktime"
              data="$url"
              width="360" height="240">
              <param name="autoplay" value="true" />
              <param name="controller" value="true" />
            </object>
            <!--<![endif]-->
          </object>
OBJECT;
  }
  else {
    $variables['object'] = l($file['filename'], $url);
  }
}
```

Thanks to the good folks at *A List Apart*, in the article *Bye Bye Embed* by Elizabeth Castro (at `http://www.alistapart.com/articles/byebyeembed`), we see how to ensure our Quicktime movie will be displayed properly on all compatible browsers. Using a conditional statement will allow any other file types to be displayed using the default link originally provided by the module.

> Note the `<<<OBJECT ... OBJECT;` notation: This PHP notation allows us to insert HTML without needing to worry about whether to escape a quote, and keeping an HTML block easily visible. `OBJECT` could be any keyword of our choice.

Thumbnail Overlays

Next, we will go to the actual display of our thumbnails. Ensure that you have an Imagecache preset of **Scale and Crop** (for which we're using 360x240 for this example). You'll browse first to **Administer | Site Building | Imagecache Presets** at `/admin/build/imagecache` and add the appropriate preset. Then you'll go to your content type display settings at **Administer | Content management | Content types | Cartoon | Display** (at `/admin/content/node-types/cartoon/display`), and set your **Cartoon Thumbnail** display on both **Teaser** and **Full** to **<Hidden>**. (Yes, you read that right. We'll be adding that back manually.)

We'll now add a new `$thumbnail` variable to our preprocess hook. We'll add the following inside the `if ($file['filemime'] == 'video/quicktime')` conditional statement block, just below the line that reads `OBJECT;`:

```
$node = node_load($file['nid']);
if ($node->field_cartoon_thumbnail[0]['filepath']) {
    $variables['thumbnail'] = theme('imagecache', 'cartoon-overlay',
$node->field_cartoon_thumbnail[0]['filepath']);
    drupal_add_js(path_to_theme() .'/thumbnail-overlay.js',
'theme');
    }
```

We're going to override the template file, which becomes slightly more complex. Note that `$id` and `$zebra` are always included in template files:

```php
<?php
/**
 *  filefield_file.tpl.php
 *  This will display the file object or link for all filefields.
 *  The following variables are available:
 *    $id: The unique count of this filefield.
 *    $zebra: 'even' or 'odd'.
 *    $file: The original file object.
 *    $url: The URL to the file itself.
 *    $icon: A representative icon based on the file's mime type.
 *    $object: The HTML to display our file, as an object or link.
 *    $thumbnail: An image to click to load our file.
 */
?>
<div class="filefield-wrapper">
  <?php if ($thumbnail) : ?>
    <?php
      // Make the embedded object invisible until clicked.
      $style = 'style="display: none;"';
    ?>
    <div class="filefield-thumbnail">
      <?php print l($thumbnail, $url, array('html' => TRUE,
        'attributes' => array('id' => "filefield-file-thumbnail-$id",
        'class' => 'filefield-file-thumbnail', 'rel' =>
        "filefield-file-file-$id"))); ?>
    </div>
  <?php endif; ?>
  <div id="filefield-file-file-<?php print $id; ?>" class=
        "filefield-file clear-block" <?php print $style; ?> >
    <?php print $object; ?>
  </div>
</div>
```

Finally, of course, we'll need to create the JavaScript file referenced in the new preprocess code with the following:

```
if (Drupal.jsEnabled) {
  $(document).ready(function () {
    $('a.filefield-file-thumbnail').click(function () {
      var video = '#'+ $(this).attr('rel');
      $(this).hide();
      $(video).show();
      return false;
    });
  });
}
```

This will display our thumbnail and actual video. After the document is loaded, the video file will be hidden. When the thumbnail area is clicked by the user, the thumbnail will be hidden and the video will be displayed. This degrades nicely as well. If a browser doesn't have JavaScript, then clicking on the image will download the movie:

Flash Video Players

The downside of embedding video directly into a page is that we depend on users' browsers to use plug-ins to display the video, and many browsers will not even have that capability for some file types.

To resolve this and to give the additional benefit of site-specific skinning (which we'll explore in the next chapter), there are several Flash video players available for use. The benefit of using a Flash solution is that Flash is installed on most modern browsers already.

For the examples in this book, we're going to use the JW FLV Media Player, which is free for non-commercial use, with a small licensing fee for other uses. The player is available at the creator Jeroen Wijering's website `http://www.jeroenwijering.com/`.

However, there are alternatives that may be better suited for certain sites such as Flow Player (free, but with a non-replaceable logo without a licensing fee), Wimpy Rave (available with a license fee), and Dash Media Player (a player made specifically for Drupal, free for non-commercial use).

I am collaborating with other interested developers to create a completely open-source GPL Media Player for Drupal, which has a development version currently available at `http://drupal.org/project/media_player`. Drupal's Media Player should be available as a beta version later this year, and you can sign up for news about its progress at `http://drupalmultimedia.org`. Meanwhile, you are encouraged to use the JW FLV Media Player, as the player will be completely compatible with it, allowing for ease of migration. If the player is already available by the time you read this book, then feel free to use it for all examples in the book as it can be interchanged seamlessly.

After downloading your player, you will want to place it somewhere on your site and note the directory in which it's located. As you'll be able to designate its location later, its placement doesn't really matter. If you put it in the root directory, you'll have one less step as the **jQuery Media** module (coming right up) uses that as its default. But personally, I prefer to place the media player within `/sites/all` to make it easier to check into an SVN repository.

jQuery Media

Everyone knows how difficult it is to ensure cross-browser compatibility when displaying media. To make the job easier, I've developed a plug-in wrapper module for the **jQuery Media** plug-in by Mike Alsup. The module, also named **jQuery Media**, is available at `http://drupal.org/project/jquery_media`, and the original plug-in (included with the module) is at `http://www.malsup.com/jquery/media/`.

This plug-in will use jQuery to turn a specified media link into the appropriate embedded player displaying that media. This allows a page to be more accessible and takes care of cross-browser issues automatically.

Configuring the module is quite simple. First, you should install both it and the jQ module (available at `http://drupal.org/project/jq`). The jQ module creates a central repository for installed jQuery plug-ins, making it easier to manage and configure them.

Once installed, you first need to tell it where your media player is. Do this by visiting the **jQ** settings page at **Administer | Site configuration | jQ Plugin Administration** (at `/admin/settings/jq`) and opening the fieldset for **jQuery Media**:

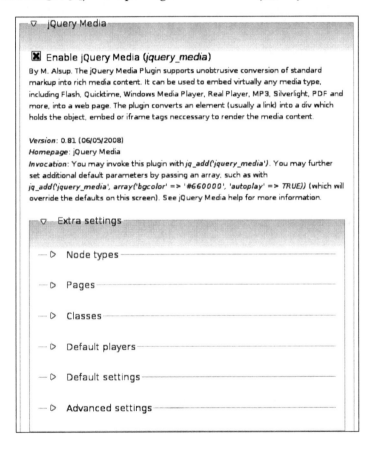

This will tell you the version of the plug-in, as well as other useful information about itself. (If you have other jQuery plug-in wrapper modules installed, they will probably also hook into this screen, allowing an overview of the jQuery that's installed and available for theming.)

You'll need to open the **Default players** fieldset and enter the file path to your media player there. Assuming we're using the JW FLV Media Player and placing it in /sites/all, we'll simply enter the full path of **sites/all/mediaplayer.swf** into the **Flash Player (flvPlayer)** text field, omitting the leading slash:

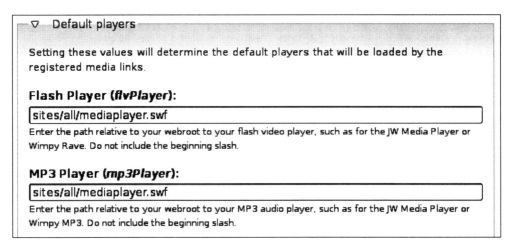

Finally, open the **Node types** fieldset on that page and check the **Cartoon** type. The module will now automatically invoke the required plug-in and properly display any video links:

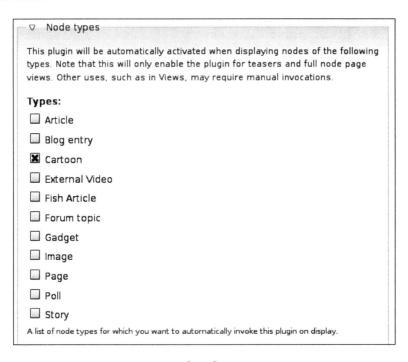

You'll also want to go to the **Default settings** of the plug-in and change the width and height to your player:

▽ Default settings

Media Width:

255

The width, in pixels, of the media that will be displayed.

Media Height:

470

The height, in pixels, of the media that will be displayed.

☑ Autoplay (*autoplay*)

If checked, then media loaded with jQuery Media will automatically start.

Background color:

#e92581

This color, in hexidecimal form (#RRGGBB), will be used as the default background color for invoked players.

Background color picker:

Click in this box to start picking your color.

Path to swfobject.js:

sites/drupal-multimedia.org/themes/dm/swfobject.js

jQuery Media will attempt to use the swfobject.js script if it is loaded. However, due to licensing requirements, that script may not be packaged in the Drupal code repository. Other modules may have need of it as well. Therefore, if you already have the script, or choose to download it from http://code.google.com/p/swfobject/, then you may enter the path to the file here, including the swfobject.js filename. Note that jQuery Media should work without this script in most cases, but using it will provide for the most optimal cross-browser experience. Do not include the beginning slash.

Logo Overlays

If you are using Flash videos that have an extension of `.flv`, you may add a logo overlay over the displayed video. To do this, we'll need to add a custom flashvar to **jQuery Media**. Open the **Advanced settings** fieldset of the **jQ** settings page and enter **sites/all/themes/mytheme/images/client-logo.png** in the **Flashvars** text field, substituting that with the path to the custom watermark you wish to use. The URL can be relative or absolute; we're just using a relative link for this example:

▽   Advanced settings

Flashvars:

sites/all/themes/mytheme/images/client-logo.png

This is a string that will be sent to the flashvars for the embedded media. An example might be *myVar1*: *'myValue1'*, *myVar2*: *'myValue2'*. Be careful when setting this, as the string is unfiltered before sending to javascript.

Params:

This is a string that will be sent to the params for the embedded media. An example might be *myParam1*: *'myValue1'*, *myParam2*: *'myValue2'*. Be careful when setting this, as the string is unfiltered before sending to javascript.

☑   Use default js file

If checked, then jQuery Media will load a js file with the defaults, rather than setting them inline. You should probably leave this unchecked while developing, so you don't need to refresh the js file, as it is created dynamically (although can be overridden below).

Default js filepath:

jquery_media.defaults.js

The path, without a leading slash, to the js file that loads the jQuery Media default settings. If it is set to the default of *jquery_media.defaults.js*, then that file will be created dynamically with the settings on this page. Once you have finished developing, you may wish to copy the output of that file to a static file and set its path here, to ensure proper caching and to reduce server load.

This allows us to create an automatic, rudimentary branding for our videos, similar to YouTube.

The **jQuery Media** module allows for more advanced usage as well, such as creating a dynamic `javascript` file for global overrides and specifying a `swfobject.js` file (which allows for even better cross-browser compatibility). Additionally, you'll have full access to the other features of the plug-in, such as automatic handling of the most commonly used media formats such as `.asf`, `.avi`, `.mov`, `.mpg`, and other video types, and audio types such as `.mp3`, `.m4a`, `.wav` (which we'll explore in the audio chapters).

Inline Local Video

You can easily use the **jQuery Media** plug-in for inline video. Simply activate the module for the node type you wish, as we did with the **Cartoon** type earlier, and add `.node .content a` to the classes. Then you would create a link to a video file within your content, and watch it being transformed.

Summary

In this chapter, we learned how to serve video from a local server using `FileField` and `jQuery` Media. We also examined some ways to customize the display, such as by adding a thumbnail splash image and a logo overlay.

In the next chapter, we'll examine some methods for file management, which canhelp making video handling just a bit easier. In particular, we'll examine threeuseful modules, including Node Reference (which can be used to link video, image,and audio node types to other nodes), Asset (which gives an easy-to-use interfacefor asset management), and Media Mover (which helps to process and store mediafiles, allowing for such things as e-mail harvesting and transforming videos to a Flash video file format)

7
File Asset Management

We're going to spend some time in this chapter dealing with file asset management. Having a good workflow and system for file management is a requirement for many larger sites, and is useful even for blogs.

As media handling in Drupal has matured, so has asset management. However, because the Drupal core currently does little to help in this regard, several contributed modules have emerged to fill the gap.

In fact, a common complaint among developers for Drupal is that the core file handling (as of Drupal 6) is inadequate to the task of managing file assets, causing it to be a tedious and contradictory process. For instance, we already saw the conflicts between how **Image** nodes and **Image fields** are handled, and the difficulty of sharing files between them (which are mitigated by several contributed modules).

There are plans in place to fix this in Drupal 7, such as the proposed hook_file patch (at http://drupal.org/node/142995). Meanwhile, several competing modules have attempted to implement their own unique file handling.

Although some modules are specific to specific media and even specific site configurations, such as **Image Attach** for **Image** nodes, there are others that are more generic and flexible.

Node Referenced Files

The **Node Reference** module, distributed with the **CCK,** allows the creation of a field that references another node. Although it may not be initially obvious how this could help us with our need for file management, it can actually be used as a powerful and simple solution.

If we think of some of the node types we've created throughout this book as wrappers for our media, this solution should become clearer. For instance, we could use a **Node Reference** to manage **Audio** nodes, allowing audio clips to be easily associated with articles.

To illustrate how this can be used, we'll pretend that our client The Hog Blog wants its articles to occasionally display videos, and have all posted videos available in a gallery.

To this end, we'll create a video type using the **Embedded Media Field**. We'll be able to create a simple view for the gallery page that simply displays all videos sorted by creation date. Then the **Article** content type will contain a node reference to our video.

You'll first need to activate the **Node Reference** module, which is included with **CCK**. If you haven't already, create a **Video** content type with a field named **field_video_reference** from **Embedded Media Field**. Finally, create an **Article** content type with a **Node reference** field called **Video reference**, with a **Select list** widget type:

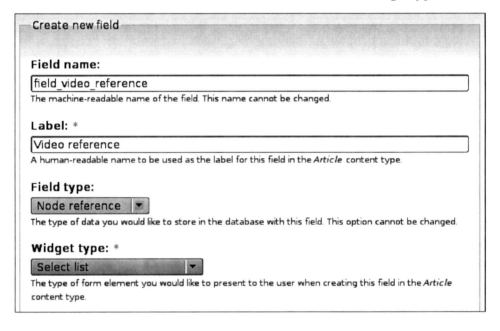

The **Select list** widget will display a list of all titles of the referenced node type(s) when creating new content. In many situations, particularly where you expect to have more than a couple of dozen nodes of that type, the **Autocomplete Text Field** widget is probably more useful as the complete list of matched nodes can easily become unwieldy. In that case, you would simply type a few characters of the video title, and it would appear in a drop-down selection list of suggested similar titles.

Make sure to check the **Video** box in the **Content types that can be referenced** section of the **Field** settings page.

> Another useful trick here is to create a view for your reference selection. By opening the **Advanced – Nodes that can be referenced (View)** fieldset, you'll be able to select a **View** that will filter the available references. For instance, you might create a **View** that lists the 20 most recent videos, and use that **View** here. That is useful in many production settings, where editors don't want to remember the title of a video they might want, don't want to sort through a hundred node titles, and are only working with recent content.

Next go to the **Display** fields page of the **Article** type by browsing to **Administer | Content management | Content types | Video | Display fields** (at `admin/content/node-type/video/display`), and select the desired settings. In our example, we'll set the **Label** of our **Video reference** field to **<Hidden>**, the selector for **Teaser** to **Teaser**, and the selector for **Full node** to **Full node**. If you've also set the display settings for the **Video** field of the **Video** content type appropriately, you'll get a thumbnail or preview-size video for the teaser, and a full-sized video, perhaps with **Autoplay**, for the full-size video node, and these will be reflected in the reference:

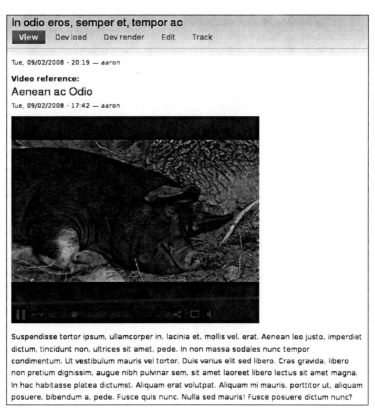

Theming Node Referenced Videos

As you see can see in the screenshot, we have a slight problem with the display. Our referenced video includes some extraneous information such as the submission date and author. This will be true when it's set to display as a teaser or full node, so we'll need to override the theme to get it displayed properly.

Other than the submission information, we want the video display to be the same as it currently is for full node and teaser displays. However, when displayed within our articles, we want a preview-size video to be displayed with a title linking to the video node below it.

To do this, we need to discover the theme function to override when displaying our node teaser. Using either **Theme Developer** or simply digging into the **Node Reference** module source code, we learn that it's either `theme_nodereference_formatter_full` or `theme_nodereference_formatter_teaser`, as appropriate.

The chosen module actually implements the two theme functions with one function, as seen here:

```
/**
 * Implementation of hook_theme().
 */
function nodereference_theme() {
  return array(
    // skipping several definitions until...
    'nodereference_formatter_full' => array(
      'arguments' => array('element'),
      'function' => 'theme_nodereference_formatter_full_teaser',
    ),
    'nodereference_formatter_teaser' => array(
      'arguments' => array('element'),
      'function' => 'theme_nodereference_formatter_full_teaser',
    ),
  );
}
```

Counter-intuitively, rather than simply overriding `theme_nodereference_formatter_full_teaser`, we'll need to implement two overrides. This is because both `theme('nodereference_formatter_full')` and `theme('nodereference_formatter_teaser')` will call back the same function, `theme_nodereference_formatter_full_teaser`.

However, taking a cue from that module rather than duplicating code, we'll create a helper function that is _phptemplate_nodereference_formatter_full_teaser. It will be called from both overrides with an added $op variable to help separate the functionality.

Add the following to template.php:

```
/**
 *  Helper function to format node reference videos.
 *  If the field is field_video, then we'll display the video
 *  or thumbnail appropriately.
 *  Otherwise, we'll return the default teaser or full display
 *  of the referenced node.
 */
function _phptemplate_nodereference_formatter_full_teaser($element,
$op) {
  $output = '';
  if (!empty($element['#item']['nid']) && is_numeric($element['#item'
]['nid'])) {
    $node = node_load($element['#item']['nid']);
    if ($node->type != 'video') {
      return theme_nodereference_formatter_full_teaser($element);
    }
    $output .= '<div class="video">';
    $output .= content_format('field_video', $node->field_video[0],
($op == 'teaser' ? 'video_thumbnail' : 'default'), $node);
    $output .= '</div>';
  }
  return $output;
}

/**
 *  Override theme('nodereference_formatter_teaser').
 */
function phptemplate_nodereference_formatter_teaser($element) {
  return _phptemplate_nodereference_formatter_full_teaser($element,
'teaser');
}

/**
 *  Override theme('nodereference_formatter_full').
 */
function phptemplate_nodereference_formatter_full($element) {
  return _phptemplate_nodereference_formatter_full_teaser($element,
'full');
}
```

Asset Module

Our newest client is a sports television network that offers private video content to its paying Internet users. There are editors for each covered sport, such as for synchronized swimming, full-contact badminton, and speed chess. They want to allow the editor of each sport to manage their own video files. Additionally, there will be a core set of generic videos that may be used globally. Editors should be able to easily access, upload, and embed any videos owned by them, and any videos that have been added to the global set. Because the users pay for this premium service, we need to be able to control access to videos, allowing only users of a certain role to be able to view them.

After browsing the contributed modules project pages of Drupal, we discover a likely candidate to handle this task: the **Asset** module. The **Asset** module adds an API to create a new file system for Drupal, which also creates an intuitive and easy-to-use UI for editors and administrators. It also allows files to be controlled by public or private access.

Let's activate the **Asset** module. There are other available and useful related modules as well, but we won't cover them in this section.

 Note that I am taking a risk by including the **Asset** module in this book, as it is not upgraded to Drupal 6 at the time of this writing. The module's maintainers have stated plans to upgrade it soon, so hopefully that will have happened by the time this goes to the press. Hopefully, little will have changed for the UI, although there's always a chance of differences. Obviously, the documentation of the module should be followed when there is a discrepancy.

Next, create a new node type with an **Asset** field. We'll add content from this type and see something like the following:

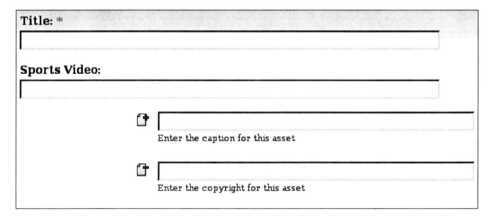

Clicking on the icon that looks like a page with a green plus sign, you will be presented with a pop-up window where you can browse your current file assets, select a video, and/or upload a new video:

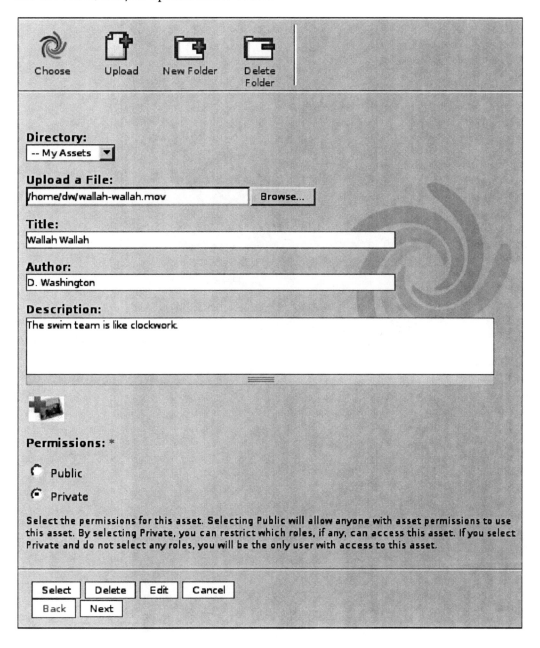

As you can see here, you can **Upload** a file from this interface as well as select an existing file with specific folders for each user:

After selecting this, the fields for your node should be filled in properly:

Submit Sports Video

Title: *

Wallah Wallah Swim Team

Sports Video:

wallah-wallah.mov

Media placeholder

Wallah Wallah
Enter the caption for this asset

D. Washington
Enter the copyright for this asset

Note that this module intends to be all-encompassing for media, and can handle images, video, and audio. It currently takes advantage of some external module APIs such as from **ImageCache** and **Embedded Media Field**.

Media Mover

The next possibility we'll cover is another suite of related modules called **Media Mover**. This is an API meant to handle various media types such as video and audio. The module doesn't do much on its own; it's only in conjunction with its related modules that it can be useful.

As does the **Asset** module, this module conceptualizes file handling differently than it is currently implemented in the core of Drupal. In particular, it provides hooks for harvest, process, storage, and complete configuration. This powerful API allows other modules to hook into and take advantage of that workflow.

Again, the caveat here is that the **Media Mover** module, at the time of this writing, is available only for Drupal 5. However, it is such a powerful and useful module that I hope the module will be ported soon. All screenshots and instructions are for the Drupal 5 version, which should hopefully not change too dramatically for Drupal 6.

Media Mover Processes

Harvest, in the sense of **Media Mover**, determines where files are selected from. This allows you to upload files through the browser, FTP them directly to your files directory, or even email a video from your mobile phone.

Process, as defined by **Media Mover**, will alter your files in some form similar to the **ImageCache** module. For instance, you can truncate your video files or convert them to Flash video files (assuming you have the FFmpeg library installed in PHP).

Storage determines where your files will live. This might be in your Drupal files directory, but it could just as easily be an external solution such as Amazon S3.

Finally, the **complete configuration** in **Media Mover** triggers actions to take place once a configuration has been complete. As with **Actions** and **Triggers** in Drupal 6, this allows you to do things such as setting a node's status.

Media Mover in Action

Enable the **Media Mover API**, **E-Mail Media Mover**, and **Media Mover Node** modules. This will define some basic behavior, which we will use to create a new workflow for our videos. You will also need the **Mailhandler** module installed and enabled for the e-mail harvesting functionality (available at `http://drupal.org/project/mailhandler`).

We would like to be able to email a video from our mobile phone and have it automatically attached to a new blog post.

Go to **Administer | Media Mover | Add Config** (at `/admin/media_mover/config/add`), and enter a name and description for our new configuration:

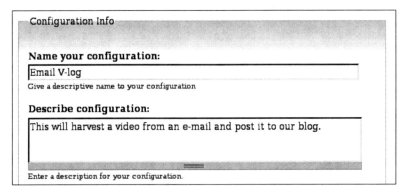

Next, you will select **Harvest email content: Harvest attachments from an email account** from the select field for **Select which** *harvest* **module and action to use**, and fill in the fields that appear:

harvest configuration

Harvesting is where files are selected from

Select which *harvest* module and action to use:

Harvest email content: Harvest attachements from an email account. ▼

Email Harvest Configuration

Allowed File Types:

mov, mp4, mp3, avi, 3gp, 3g2, divx, xvid, wmv, asf, mpg, mpeg, mpeg4, jpeg

A list of allowed file types, separated by a comma

E-mail address:

videos@example.com

The e-mail address to which users should send their submissions.

Folder:

INBOX

Optional. The folder where the mail is stored. If you want this mailbox to read from a local folder, give the full path. Leave domain, port, name, and pass empty below. Remember to set the folder to readable and writable by the webserver.

POP3 or IMAP Mailbox:

POP3 ▼

If you wish to retrieve mail from a POP3 or IMAP mailbox instead of a Folder, select POP3 or IMAP. Also, complete the Mailbox items below.

Mailbox domain:

mail.example.com

The domain of the server used to collect mail.

Mailbox port:

110

The port of the mailbox used to collect mail (usually 110 for POP3, 143 for IMAP).

Mailbox username:

videos

This username is used while logging into this mailbox during mail retrieval.

Mailbox password:

nopeeking

The password corresponding to the username above. Consider using a non-vital password, since this field is stored without encryption in the database.

Extra commands:

Optional. In some circumstances you need to issue extra commands to connect to your mail server (e.g. "/notls", "/novalidate-cert" etc.). See documentation for imap_open. Begin the string with a "/", separating each subsequent command with another "/".

Mime preference:

HTML ▼

When a user sends an e-mail containing both HTML and plain text parts, use this part as the node body.

Send error replies:

◯ Disabled

◉ Enabled

Send helpful replies to all unsuccessful e-mail submissions. Consider disabling when a listserv posts to this mailbox.

Default commands:

A set of commands which are added to each message. One command per line. See <a href="/admin /help/mailhandler/%2523commands">Commands</a>.

Signature separator:

--

All text after this string will be discarded. A typical value is "-- " that is two dashes followed by a blank in an otherwise empty line. Leave blank to include signature text in nodes.

☐ Delete messages after they are processed?

Uncheck this box to leave read messages in the mailbox. They will not be processed again unless they become marked as unread.

▷ Input format

We will leave the Process configuration alone for now. But we could easily convert our video files to Flash videos here, assuming we have the FFmpeg library installed with PHP.

Next, set the **storage configuration** to **Save data as a node**, attaching it to a **Blog entry** (assuming we have the core **Blog** module enabled; this could be any node type):

---

storage configuration

Storage is where files are stored in addition to Media Mover's internal storage

Select which *storage* module and action to use:

Media Mover node module: Save data as a node ▼

Node storage configuration

This module will try to do a best guess of harvested data and save this to a node.

Default node type:

Blog entry ▼

Save the harvested and processed data on this node type

☑ **Save files to node attachments**

If this is checked, all files harvested will be attached to the node (and potentially visable to users). If not, files will be accessible via Media Mover.

☐ **Data override**

If this is checked, all saved nodes will have the title an author set below.

Default author:

anonymous ○

If a user is not passed in, this will be the default author.

Default title:

If a title is not passed in, this will be the default node title.

Finally, we can set our node status in the **Completion Configuration** and be ready to send some videos to our blog:

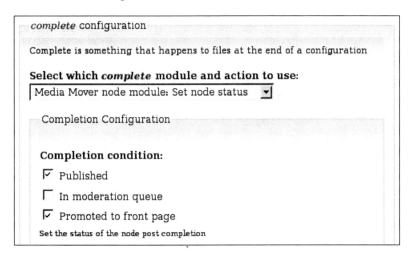

Press **Save configuration** to finish. The resulting screen will show an **Overview** of all **Media Mover** configurations. If we click on the run link from that screen, we will harvest new files from our email and create new blog entries. Or we can just wait for cron to do it for us:

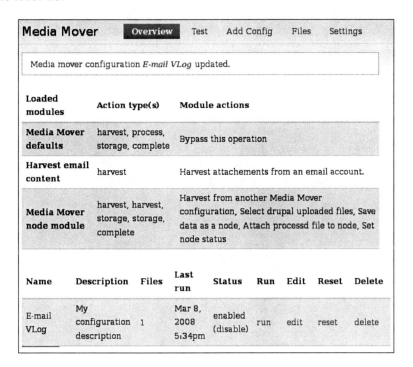

Note that both the **Asset** module and **Media Mover** are quite powerful, with much more functionality than we were able to cover in this chapter. They are both worth examining to see if they offer solutions for your specific needs.

Kaltura

Finally, there are also external solutions to file management that may be considered, depending on the needs for a site. Notably, **Kaltura,** which has partnered with the Wikimedia Foundation to develop video wiki software for the Mediawiki platform, offers an off-site video, image, and audio mixer. It can be used to store, manage, and mix various media. It is currently developing a module to integrate its free and low-cost service into Drupal.

Available at `http://kaltura.com/`, this open source solution is capable of managingmedia files for a site, including bulk upload, encoding, transcoding, and import. Italso may be used to edit and remix multimedia, creating new videos from uploadedmedia or content imported from public sources available from the Kaltura network.

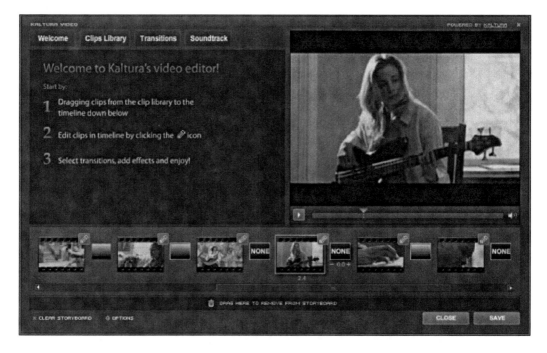

Summary

In this chapter, we explored options for managing our media. First, by harnessing the power of **Node Reference**, we brought Drupal fully under our control. This allowed us to embed provided media within our nodes, while at the same time making it available outside that node such as for galleries. We also explored the **Asset** module as a full-featured solution. Finally, we touched briefly on **Media Mover**, which is a framework for harvesting, processing, and storing our site's media.

As a general reminder, you are encouraged to become active in the development of your favorite module: by examining the relevant issue queues; by helping to review, test, and even write patches; by writing and offering documentation and tutorials; and by contacting the module developers to find out how else you can help.

In the next few chapters, we'll learn how to wisely include and embed audio within our sites.

8
Audio Nodes

Audio has sometimes been the forgotten step-child of multimedia, and this has in the past been reflected in Drupal. Because the Internet has largely been a visual experience, there has not been much sound. Also due to the nature of the evolution of browsers, computer sound handling, and the fact that users of the Web are accustomed to viewing content using the concept of pages of a book, support for audio has been spotty in general, far before Drupal ever came along.

By the end of this chapter, you will have seen how to overcome some of the apparent limitations of including audio in your content.

Audio Formats

As with video, there are a multitude of audio file formats available. However, what to use is limited by the player(s) you wish to support on your site. The **Audio** module (which we'll cover in this chapter) by default allows `.wav`, `.mp3`, and `.ogg` files, so we'll examine those briefly. There are other formats you might need to use as well such as `.mp4`, `.wma`, or `.ra`. We'll jump back into this topic in the next chapter, since these formats may require special handling.

WAV Lossless Format

The first format, WAV, is one of the few formats that don't compress their data. This means that the sound quality will be highest, but it also means that the file size will be large. In general, this format is used for short audio samples that require high fidelity, and will usually result in files too large for the bandwidth required for anything more than a few seconds in length.

MP3 for Music

Most users will be familiar with the MP3 file format, which is reputed for storing and sharing music. The format is widely supported by many players, both commercial and open source. Sound compressed with an MP3 encoder will result in a file size about a tenth the size of its uncompressed WAVcounterpart, and will usually be of a quality acceptable to most users, other than audiophiles. When encoding sound into MP3, the creator is able to choose the quality and compression rate.

Open Source OGG

The MP3 compression algorithm is actually proprietary, with several companies claiming to own the relevant licenses. Although MP3 is the de facto standard for audio in most cases and may be used with most open source encoders, the OGG format was developed as an open source alternative. It is actually a wrapper for several compression algorithms, including lossless and compressed formats.

Encoding Audio

There are many commercial and open source options available for encoding sound files. What you use depends on many factors, including operating system, source of the sound, familiarity, and compatibility of the output with the final player being used. Rather than going into some options here, as that is out of the intended scope of this book, you are directed to an Internet search for audio encoders, audio codecs, and audio software. As there are literally hundreds of great options, you'll probably want to try a few until you settle on the one that works best for you.

Audio Module

By far, the easiest solution is the `Audio` module that has been a staple of Drupal developers for years. For most requirements, this module works fine out of the box even with its inherent limitations.

The module creates a node type, aptly called Audio. For our first example, we'll use this to create audio clips of selected speakers from our local rotary club.

Download and install the `Audio` module from `http://drupal.org/project/audio`. You will also need the `Views` and `Token` modules, available from `http://drupal.org/project/views/` and `http://drupal.org/project/token/` respectively.

Assuming your user role has the permissions (which you might first need to set at **Administer | User management | Access control**, at `/admin/user/access`), you will be able to add audio nodes with no further configuration.

To automatically fill in metadata such as a track's title and artist, you will also want to enable the **Audio getID3** module, which requires the **getID3** module from `http://drupal.org/project/getid3`. In turn, `getID3` requires the third-party `getID3` library available at `http://getID3.org`. Create a `getid3` folder within `/sites/all/modules/getid3`, and extract the entire library into that folder. You'll go to the **getID3 settings** page by browsing to **Administer | Site configuration | getID3** (at `/admin/settings/getid3`) to ensure you have the correct version.

> When you go to the **getID3 settings** page, you might see a warning that reads **Your getID3 library is insecure! The demos distributed with getID3 contains code which creates a huge security hole. Remove the demos directory (/sites/all/modules/getid3/getid3/demos) from beneath Drupal's directory.** You need to remove the entire `/demos` folder from the new `getid3` folder to maintain your site's security.

Submitting Audio Content

Go to **Create content | Submit Audio** (at `/node/add/audio`). You will notice first that unlike other node types, the **Title** field of the node is already filled with content: **[audio-tag-title-raw] by [audio-tag-artist-raw]**:

Submit Audio

Title: *

[audio-tag-title-raw] by [audio-tag-artist-raw]

The title can use the file's metadata. You can use the tokens listed below to insert information into the title. **Note:** the node title is escaped so it is safe to use the -raw tokens.

▷ Token list

This will attempt to create a title automatically according to the information included in the audio file, assuming the file offers that information, as is usually the case with MP3 files. This will happen after the content's submission and you may, of course, put whatever you wish in the node's title. If present in the metadata, the file's **Title by Artist** will be auto-generated using the **[audio-tag-title-raw]** and **[audio-tag-artist-raw]** tags to substitute the relevant text.

Leave this alone for now, and press **Browse** in the **Add a new audio file** section. This will allow you to browse through your local files to find an audio file to upload. Send an MP3 and press **Submit**:

▽   Audio File Info

Current File:
No file is attached.

Add a new audio file:

| | Browse... |

Click "Browse..." to select an audio file to upload. Only files with the following extensions are allowed: *mp3 wav ogg*.
NOTE: the current PHP configuration limits uploads to *2 MB*.

☑ Allow file downloads.
If checked, a link will be displayed allowing visitors to download this audio file on to their own computer.
WARNING: even if you leave this unchecked, clever users will be able to find a way to download the file. This just makes them work a little harder to find the link.

You may get a message that reads: **A file must be provided. If you tried uploading a file, make sure it's less than the upload size limit.** If so, it may be because the PHP file upload size limit is too low for the file you are uploading. You will see that limit in a note below the **Add a new audio file** text field, and also at the top of the **Audio settings** page at **Administer | Site configuration | Audio settings** (/admin/settings/audio). You will need to adjust upload_max_filesize and post_max_size with a php_value directive in your site's .htaccess file or php.ini file. (For instance, you might enter php_value upload_max_filesize 4M and php_value post_max_size 4M on different lines in one of the two files.) If neither of those changes works, you will need to contact your web host provider.

If you get a message reading **Artist field is required, Title field is required,** or **The Audio getid3 module cannot find the getID3 library used to read and write ID3 tags,** then either the Audio getID3 module has not been installed, or the file you're uploading doesn't have the relevant metadata information. You'll be able to manually add (or override) any of the metadata after submitting the node:

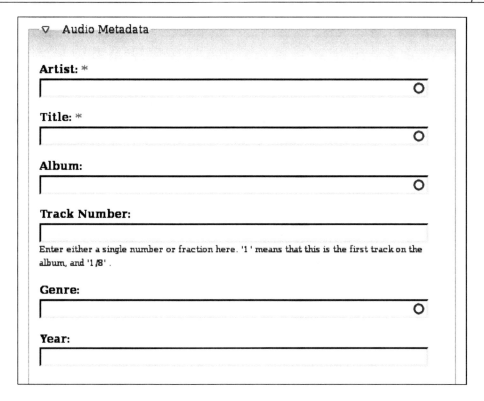

After submitting an audio file, users will be able to play the file from the page without any further configuration. Additionally, users may download the file from the relevant link, unless you unchecked **Allow file downloads** when submitting the node:

Metadata

The **Audio** node stores other relevant data about the audio file as well such as the
Length and the **Bitrate**. This data is automatically extracted from the audio files.
Some of this, such as the **File Size**, is basic file information stored for any file, while
other data, such as the **Artist** or **Album**, is stored within the file in the form of
metadata. You can view the information available for a file when editing the node:

▽　Audio File Info

This file information was loaded from the file by the getID3 library.

Current File	files.dm/audio/Blackthorn_Stick.mp3
Play count	1
Download count	0
Format	mp3
File Size	1,249,742 bytes
Length	1:18
Sample rate	44,100 Hz
Channel mode	Stereo
Bitrate	128,000 bytes/second
Bitrate mode	CBR

Replace this with a new file:

[   ] Browse...

Click "Browse..." to select an audio file to upload. Only files with the following extensions are
allowed: *mp3 wav ogg*.
NOTE: the current PHP configuration limits uploads to *2 MB*.

☑ Allow file downloads.

If checked, a link will be displayed allowing visitors to download this audio file on to their own
computer.
WARNING: even if you leave this unchecked, clever users will be able to find a way to
download the file. This just makes them work a little harder to find the link.

From the **Audio settings** page (browse to **Administer | Site configuration | Audio settings,** at /admin/settings/audio), you can set up the default tokens to use when creating the node's title and teaser:

Audio settings

| **Audio** | getID3 | Metadata tags | Players |

The current PHP configuration limits file uploads to *2 MB*.

There are two PHP ini settings, upload_max_filesize and post_max_size, that limit the maximum size of uploads. You can change these settings in the php.ini file or by using a php_value directive in Apache .htaccess file. Consult the PHP documentation for more info.

[more help...]

Default node title format:

[audio-tag-title-raw] by [audio-tag-artist-raw]

The audio node's title can use the file's metadata as variables. This will be used as the default title for all new audio nodes. By using the tokens listed below, you can automatically create titles from things like a song's artist or title. **Note:** the node title is escaped so it is safe to use the -raw tokens.

Node teaser format:

[audio-player]
[audio-length]

Use this setting to customize the teasers for audio nodes. Using the tokens listed below you can select what information about the file will be displayed. **Note: the teaser is not escaped so it is unsafe to use the -raw tokens.**

▷ List of available tokens

Permitted audio file extensions:

mp3 wav ogg

Audio file extensions that users can upload. Separate extensions with a space and do not include a leading dot.

☑ Downloadable by default

Check this to make downloadable the default setting for new audio nodes. You should be aware that even when audio is not marked as downloadable, clever users can still download it, this just makes the work harder.

| Save configuration | | Reset to defaults |

By default, the title is **[audio-tag-title-raw] by [audio-tag-artist-raw]**, and the teaser is **[audio-player]
[audio-length]**. You can see a list of all tokens available by clicking on the **List of available tokens**. For instance, **[audio-player]** will display the player used to play the audio output, **[audio-tag-year]** will display the year stored in the metadata, and **[audio-file-size]** will display the file size in bytes. You'll have the full power of the **Token** module for this. So, you could also have the title display the date, the node submitted, or a term from its vocabulary.

You also have full control of what metadata tags will be stored and displayed by browsing to **Administer | Site configuration | Audio settings | Metadata tags** (at /admin/settings/audio/metadata). Here you'll see a list of tags stored by default, including **artist**, **title**, **album**, **track**, **genre**, and **year**. You can easily add to and delete from these on this page:

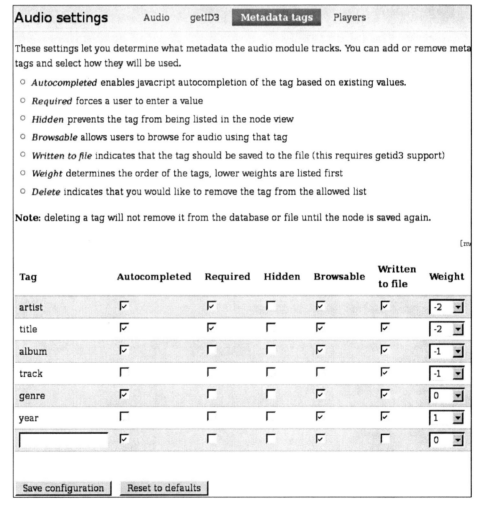

You may also change the other options as desired. If a tag is marked as **Autocompleted**, then if you manually enter a tag when submitting a new audio node, the field will attempt to autocomplete your selection from other nodes already in place. If set to **Required**, you may not submit the node without entering a value. If **Hidden**, then the tag won't be displayed to the user. The **Browsable** option will create a listing page for this tag using a **View**. When **Written to file**, the tag will be saved in the MP3 file, overwriting any information stored previously in the metadata. **Weight** determines the order of tags, and **Delete** is used to remove one from the listing entirely.

Audio Players

The Audio module ships with two Flash players out of the box for a total of four viewing formats. The first, the **XSPF Web Music Player**, created by Fabricio Zuardi at http://musicplayer.sourceforge.net/ comes with three formats: **Extended**, **Button**, and **Slim**. The **1pixelout Flash player** was written by Martin Laine originally for WordPress, at http://www.1pixelout.net/code/audio-player-wordpress-plugin/. You can choose which player to use by browsing to **Administer | Site configuration | Audio settings | Players** (at /admin/settings/audio/players):

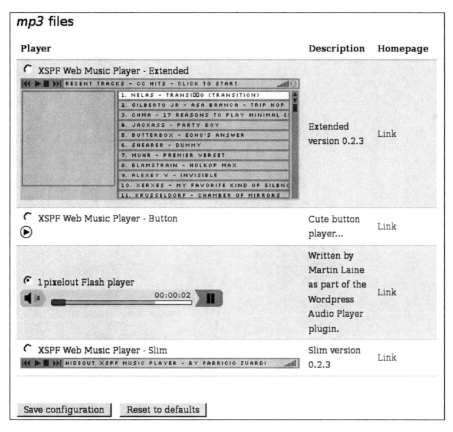

Summary

This chapter has largely been an excursion into the Audio module. We have learned how to easily create **Audio** nodes, displaying our sound and music files within the content of our sites.

In the following chapters, we will learn how to take more control of our audio, including expanding our repertoire of available players, using jQuery to better control the output, and examining options for streaming audio.

9
Audio Fields

In this chapter, we'll toss out the **Audio** module work we did earlier. Though this is a useful module if you want to have an easily configured solution, in many situations, there are some benefits from using the **FileField** module instead. It's light-weight, it's flexible, and it's easy to customize. It may also be easier to add support for players other than the **1PixelOut** and **XSPF** players distributed with Audio.

Additionally, as of this writing, the Drupal 6 version of the **Audio** module wasn't quite ready for production. But I am confident it will be soon, if not already.

Finally, there may be specific reasons for wanting to choose a **FileField** solution over the **Audio** module. Similar to the quandary of whether to use the **Image** module or **Image Field**, the most common reason would probably be to allow multiple audio files to be attached to a node, or to allow audio fields to be associated with other types of nodes. (Note that the **Audio** module is also bundled with the **Audio Attach** module, which might be a solution for that as well.)

FileField Remixed

We examined **FileField** in the chapters about Video. If you haven't already done so, you'll need to download the **FileField** module from `http://drupal.org/project/filefield` and enable it on the **Modules** administration page (by browsing to **Administer | Site building | Modules**, at `/admin/build/modules`).

Now create a new content type named **Album** by going to **Administer | Content management | Content types | Add content type** (at `/admin/content/types/add`). We'll next add a **FileField** to this by editing the new **Album** type and selecting the **Add field** tab (at `/admin/content/types/album/add_field`). Call it **Song**, select the **File** for the **Field type**, press **Continue**, and press **Continue** again (leaving the **Widget type** as File Upload).

In the **Permitted upload file extensions**, enter **mp3** for now.

If you wish, you may enter a new **File path** as well such as **audio**. Uploaded files would then be saved to that path. Note that you have access to the **Token** module's features here. So, for instance you may enter something like **audio/[user-raw]**, which will replace **[user-raw]** with the username of the node's creator:

Permitted upload file extensions:

mp3

Extensions a user can upload to this field. Separate extensions with a space and do not include the leading dot. Leaving this blank will allow users to upload a file with any extension.

▽ File size restrictions

Limits for the size of files that a user can upload. Note that these settings only apply to newly uploaded files, whereas existing files are not affected.

Maximum upload size per file:

Specify the size limit that applies to each file separately. Enter a value like "512" (bytes), "80K" (kilobytes) or "50M" (megabytes) in order to restrict the allowed file size. If you leave this this empty the file sizes will be limited only by PHP's maximum post and file upload sizes.

Maximum upload size per node:

Specify the total size limit for all files in field on a given node. Enter a value like "512" (bytes), "80K" (kilobytes) or "50M" (megabytes) in order to restrict the total size of a node. Leave this empty if there should be no size restriction.

▽ Path settings

File path:

audio/[user-raw]

Optional subdirectory within the *"files"* directory where files will be stored. Do not include trailing slash.

Token	Replacement value
User tokens	
[user]	User's name
[user-raw]	User's unfiltered name. WARNING - raw user input.
[uid]	User's ID

Finally, select **Unlimited** for the **Number of values**, since we'll allow a single album to contain many songs. We'll also check the **Required** checkbox so that each album will hold at least one song. Finally, we will ensure that the **Default listed value** is **Listed**, and that we select the **Enforce Default** radio button for **How should the list value be handled?** This will force a node to always list files when displayed. We need to list our files, although we plan ultimately to control display of an album's songs in the player:

Global settings

These settings apply to the *Song* field in every content type in which it appears.

☒ Required

Number of values:

[Unlimited ▼]

Maximum number of values users can enter for this field.
'Unlimited' will provide an 'Add more' button so the users can add as many values as they like.
Warning! Changing this setting after data has been created could result in the loss of data!

Default list value: *

⦿ Listed

◯ Hidden

The list option determines whether files are visible on node views. This will be used as the default value for the list option.

How should the list value be handled?: *

◯ User Configurable. (Users will be able to set the list value per file.)

⦿ Enforce Default. (The default list value will be used for all files, and the list checkbox will not be displayed to users.)

Description field:

◯ Disabled

⦿ Enabled

When enabled, will display a text field where users may enter a description about the uploaded file.

Now we can add an album node with a few songs by going to **Create content |
Album** (at /node/add/album). Uploading is simple, although we may have the same
PHP file size limitations as described in the previous chapter:

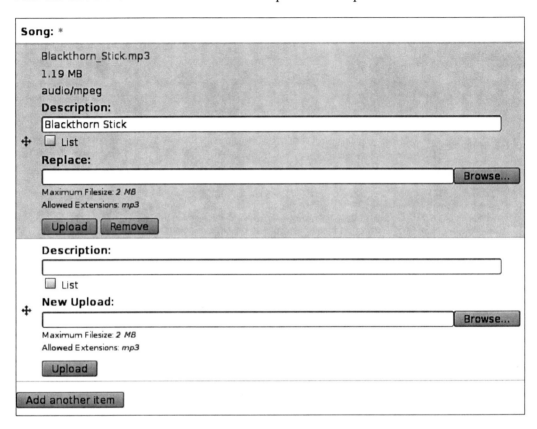

At this point, we only have a link displayed for our files. Our next task is to create an
inline player for the audio. One possibility would be to override the theme function.
However, we have other tools available that will make our job easier and even
ensure cross-browser compatibility, better accessibility, and valid HTML:

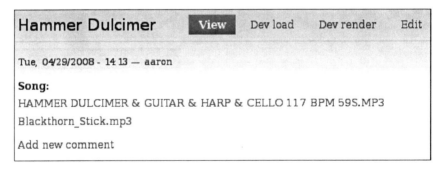

jQuery Media to the Rescue

The **jQuery Media** plug-in, written by Mike Alsup at `http://www.malsup.com/jquery/media/`, is a perfect solution. It will convert any link to media into the browser-specific code required for displaying the media. The **jQuery Media** module is a configurable wrapper for this plug-in. We covered this briefly in the chapters about Video, but this module works well for audio as well.

We'll also need a media player. For this exercise, we'll again use the **JW FLV Media Player** developed by Jeroen Wijering. This excellent player is free for non-commercial use, and has a very inexpensive licensing fee for other uses.

First, download that player from `http://jeroenwijering.com/` and install the `player.swf` file somewhere in your site's directory tree. If you install it in the site's www root folder, the module will work with little extra configuration. But you can install it in the files directory, your theme folder, or another convenient place if you need it for your environment. Just remember where you put it for future reference.

Next, download and enable the **jQuery Media** module from `http://drupal.org/project/jquery_media`. You may wish to also install the **jQ** module from `http://drupal.org/project/jq`, which consolidates jQuery plug-ins installed on your site.

The configuration is simple, and is covered in more detail in the earlier chapters. You'll just need to enter the filepath of your media player, which can be different than the Flash Video player entered earlier, if desired. Go to the **jQuery Media Administration** page by browsing to **Administer | Site configuration | jQuery Media Administration** (at `/admin/settings/jquery_media`). Open the **Default players** (within **Extra settings**) and enter the filepath of your media player in the **MP3 Player (mp3Player)** text field:

▽ Default players

Setting these values will determine the default players that will be loaded by the registered media links.

Flash Player (*flvPlayer*):

sites/drupal-multimedia.org/themes/dm/wimpy.swf

Enter the path relative to your webroot to your flash video player, such as for the JW Media Player or Wimpy Rave. Do not include the beginning slash.

MP3 Player (*mp3Player*):

sites/drupal-multimedia.org/themes/dm/mediaplayer.swf

Enter the path relative to your webroot to your MP3 audio player, such as for the JW Media Player or Wimpy MP3. Do not include the beginning slash.

Now just check the **Album** box in **Node types,** and set the width and height within **Default settings**. In most cases, you would be done and the audio would be displayed automatically with no further configuration.

However, we're assuming you plan to use this module in conjunction with videos, which may have already set a width and height. That means we'll need to do some more customization.

> Note: You do not need to do any of this, unless you have video and audio files on the site both using jQuery Media. You should refer to Chapter 6: *Local Video* for more information about overriding theme preprocess functionality.

We need to change the class of our field and add a new invocation script. However, we don't want to affect the class of our existing video files. So add the following somewhere in the `phptemplate_preprocess_filefield_file` function, creating that function if necessary. (If you haven't already done that, then create `function phptemplate_preprocess_filefield_file(&$variables)` in `template.php`.

```
$node = node_load($file['nid']);
if ($node->type == 'album') {
  $variables['classes'] = 'filefield-file-song';
  if (module_exists('jquery_media')) {
    jquery_media_add(array('media class' => '.filefield-file-song
                a', 'media height' => 20, 'media width' => 200));
  }
}
else {
  $variables['classes'] = 'filefield-file';
}
```

Then you'll need to change a line in `filefield_file.tpl.php`. (If you haven't already created that file, create it in your theme directory, and copy the code from the `theme_filefield_file` function that is found in `/sites/all/modules/filefield/filefield_formater.inc`.)

The original line in question reads as follows:

```
return '<div class="filefield-file clear-block">'. $icon .
l($file['filename'], $url) .'</div>';
```

However, in Chapter 6, we rewrote that line to read:

```
<div id="filefield-file-file-<?php print $id; ?>"
class="filefield-file clear-block" <?php print $style; ?> >
```

In either case, simply replace `class="filefield-file clear-block"` with `class="<?php print $classes; ?> clear-block"`.

External Audio

As with images and videos, there are a growing number of third-party providers of audio who offer their content to be embedded on external sites. To this end, the **Embedded Audio Field** module, included in the **Embedded Media Field** package, supports several providers. In a similar method to the others in that package, you may paste the URL or embed code from a supported provider and the desired audio content will be parsed and displayed appropriately.

Download and install the **Embedded Media Field** module from `http://drupal.org/project/emfield/`. You'll also need to enable the **Embedded Audio Field**.

Create a new content type, which we'll call **EmAudio** for this example (so that it doesn't conflict with the **Audio** module, if that's installed). To do this, browse to **Content management | Content types | Add content type** (at `/admin/content/types/add`).

Next, add an **Embedded Audio/3rd Party Audio** field, also named **Embedded Audio**, by selecting that radio and pressing the **Create field** button. You can do that by editing the new content type and hitting the **Add field** tab (at `/admin/content/types/emaudio/add_field`).

On the following page, you can change any required settings. But it's OK to leave them blank for now. If you leave the **Providers** checkboxes unchecked, they'll all be supported. If you check one or more, then only those providers will be allowed for this content type:

The other sections of this page control the display of embedded audio content. You can control the size of the player, whether it will **Autoplay** during display, and how thumbnails will appear, if provided. Note that if you have **Embedded Media Thumbnail** installed, you will be able to provide custom thumbnails, in case a provider doesn't supply thumbnails with their service:

Audio Display Settings

These settings control how this audio player is displayed in its full size, which defaults to 425x350.

Audio display width: *

```
425
```

The width of the audio. It defaults to 425.

Audio display height: *

```
350
```

The height of the audio. It defaults to 350.

☐ Autoplay

If supported by the provider, checking this box will cause the audio player to automatically begin after it loads when in its full size.

Audio Preview Settings

These settings control how this audio is displayed in its preview size, which defaults to 425x350.

Audio preview width: *

```
425
```

The width of the preview audio. It defaults to 425.

Audio preview height: *

```
350
```

The height of the preview audio. It defaults to 350.

☐ Autoplay

If supported by the provider, checking this box will cause the audio player to automatically begin after it loads when in its preview size.

Thumbnail

When displayed as a thumbnail, these settings control the image returned. Note that not all 3rd party audio content providers offer thumbnails, and others may require an API key or other requirements. More information from the settings page. The default size for thumbnails is 120x90.

Audio width: *

```
120
```

The width of the thumbnail. It defaults to 120.

Thumbnail height: *

```
90
```

The height of the thumbnail. It defaults to 90.

Default thumbnail path:

```

```

Path to a local default thumbnail image for cases when a thumbnail can't be found. For example, you might have a default thumbnail at *files/thumbnail.png*.

If you're not User 1, then make certain that you have permission to add content by going to **Administer | User management | Access rules** (at /admin/user/rules), and checking **Create embedded audio content** for the desired user role.

Now, you'll just go to an external provider such as Odeo, find a podcast or clip you want to feature, and click and drag the URL to the **Embedded Audio** field of your node creation page (by browsing to /node/add/emaudio):

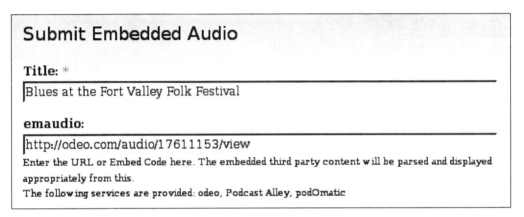

Submit your node, and you have your new podcast nicely displayed:

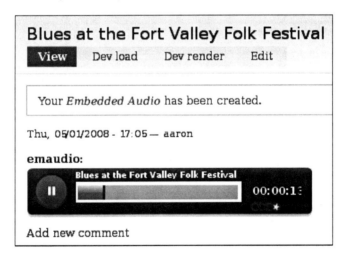

Summary

We have branched away from the **Audio** module, discovering the power of **FileField** to create custom audio fields. We have also learned to use **jQuery Media** to give better browser support. We've also explored embedding third-party audio content with **Embedded Audio Field**.

In the next chapter, we'll examine more jQuery options to give us more power when theming. We'll also take a closer look at playlist options, including creating custom user lists and using XSPF to send multiple audio sources to a player.

10
Theming Audio

At first thought, it might seem as though there is little, if any, need for a themer to do anything with an audio clip. However, as we learned in the prior chapters, there are many solutions for audio with Drupal and there are also many different ways to display audio content within a site.

For this chapter, we'll examine three ways to theme/re-theme our audio. First, we'll embed a node-referenced clip within a view of article titles. Then, we'll display a player that will play a list of clips using jQuery to synchronize a display of links with the player. Finally, we'll create user-customized playlists that can be embedded in other sites.

These techniques were recently used in the redeployment of Air America Radio's site at http://airamerica.com/, where you can see live examples:

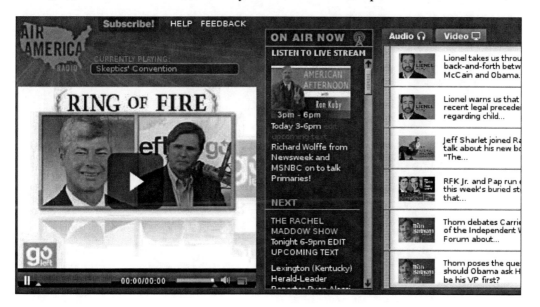

Node Referenced Clips

As has been explored with Images and Video, **Node Reference** can be a powerful module for including content within content. For instance, you might have a news site where you need to embed an audio clip within an article.

That's just what we'll do in this example. First, create a content type called **Article**, if you haven't already from an earlier chapter. (You can create new content types by browsing to **Administer | Content management | Content types** and clicking on **Add Content Type**, at `/admin/content/types/add`.) Then add another content type, called **Clip**.

We'll use a **FileField** for this example, although you could easily use another audio field type such as an **Audio Field** or an **Embedded Audio Field**. Do this by clicking on the **Clip** link of the **Content types** overview screen and then the **Add Field** tab (at **Administer | Content management | Content types | Clip | Add field**, or `/admin/content/types/clip/add_field`). Call this new **File** field **Audio Clip**. Refer to Chapter 9 if you need more help doing this. We'll set **Permitted upload file extensions** to **mp3**.

Finally, we'll go back to our **Article** content type and add a **Node Reference** field, which we'll call **Clip**. (You'll browse back to **Administer | Content management | Content types | Article | Add field** at `/admin/content/types/article/add_field` to do this.) Leave the widget at **Select List** for now. For **Content types that can be referenced**, you'll check the **Clip** type.

You can now add a few clips and articles to populate some test data:

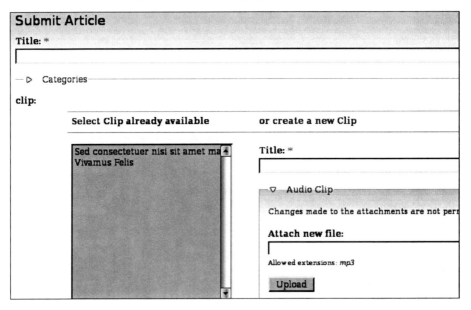

As we learned in the last chapter, we can use the **jQuery Media** module to turn the resulting link into an embedded player. Assuming that module has already been set up, you'll just need to browse to the **jQ Plugin Administration page** at **Administer | Site Configuration | jQ Plugin Administration** (/admin/settings/jq), and check the **Clip** checkbox under the **Node types** fieldset.

> Follow the instructions in Chapter 9 to download and install the **JW FLV Media Player** from http://www.jeroenwijering.com/. You'll specifically need the mediaplayer.swf file to be in your site's directory tree. Also install and configure the **jQuery Media** module from http://drupal.org/project/jquery_media following the instructions from that chapter. Again, if you are mixing video with audio on the same site, you may need to tweak your theme as explained in that chapter.

Overriding the created link will be a little tricky. It requires understanding how the link is created in the first place. We know the link from the **Article** is created with the **Node Reference** module. Examining the nodereference.module file (in /sites/all/modules/cck/modules/nodereference), we see the theme_nodereference_formatter_default function.

Taking our cue from earlier modules, we'll override this theme function using a preprocess_hook function to separate PHP development from the theme layer. When we reference clip nodes, we need to change the link's URL to the path of the file, which isn't available to our function. This means we'd have to load it manually in the function.

We'll add the following function to template.php:

```
/**
 *  implement hook_preprocess_nodereference_formatter_default.
 *  This interjects itself in the theme('nodereference_formatter_
                                                      default')
 *  structure, creating variables available for use by
 *  nodereference_formatter_default.tpl.php.
 */
function phptemplate_preprocess_nodereference_formatter_default
                                                (&$variables) {
  $variables['link'] = '';
  if (!empty($variables[0]['#item']['nid']) && is_numeric($variables
  [0]['#item']['nid']) && ($variables['title'] = _nodereference_titles
  ($variables[0]['#item']['nid'])))  {
    // Create the default link.
    $variables['url'] = 'node/'. $variables[0]['#item']['nid'];
    $variables['link'] = l($variables['title'], $variables['url']);
```

```
    // Load the referenced node.
    $variables['node'] = node_load($variables[0]['#item']['nid']);
    if ($variables['node']->type == 'clip') {
      // Load the file contained in the audio clip.
      $variables['file'] = $variables['node']->field_audio_clip[0];
      if (user_access('view filefield uploads') && is_file($variables
                                        ['file']['filepath'])) {
        // Override the $link variable created above to link to
                                                    the file.
        $path = $variables['file']['filepath'];
        $variables['url'] = file_create_url($path);
        $variables['title'] = $variables['file']['description'] ?
        $variables['file']['description'] : $variables['file']
                                                    ['filename'];
        $variables['link'] = l($variables['title'], $variables['url'],
            array('attributes' => array('class' => 'media-clip')));
        if (module_exists('jquery_media')) {
          // Add a smaller version of the player with jQuery Media.
          jquery_media_add(array('media class' => 'a.media-clip',
                    'media height' => 20, 'media width' => 200));
        }
      }
    }
  }
}
```

Then create `nodereference_formatter_default.tpl.php` in the theme directory with the following code:

```php
<?php
/**
 *  nodereference_formatter_default.tpl.php
 *  This will display either a link to the referenced node, or to its
                                file if the node is a clip.
 *  The following variables are available:
 *    $id: The unique count of this filefield.
 *    $zebra: 'even' or 'odd'.
 *    $link: The link to display.
 *    $title: The title of the link.
 *    $url: The URL path of the link.
 *    $node: The referenced node.
 *    $file: If the referenced node is a clip, then this is the audio
                                file it contains.
 */
?>
<?php print $link; ?>
```

Finally, make sure to clear your theme's cache by visiting **Administer | Site building | Themes** (at `/admin/build/themes`), and create some **Articles** referencing **Clips**:

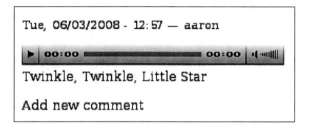

Alternatives

There are other alternatives for attaching audio files to content. Most notable is the use of the **Audio Attach** module, which is dependent on the **Audio** module. This will allow multiple Audio nodes to be associated with certain content, and will work out of the box. For many sites, this may be an easier solution. As the **Audio** module matures, it will continue to be a strong contender.

Audio Playlists

The Playlist is the audio version of a slideshow. Before continuing, we should note the multiple uses of the phrase playlist in online multimedia. The first use we're about to explore is the concept of creating a series of audio clips that may be played sequentially, often from a single embedded player, but may include a listing of audio clips on a page. The second use is to create a user-generated listing of clips, as opposed to an editor-controlled playlist, which may be presented in a similar fashion. This could be used to mark favorite clips for later playback, for instance. We will examine this later.

We already know how to create a series of audio clips that may be listed on a single page: Take the work we did in the last section with the **Clips** embedded in **Articles**, and simply mark the **Clip** node reference field as accepting more than one value (from **Administer | Content management | Content types | Article | Manage fields | Clip** at `/admin/content/node-types/clip/fields/field_audio_clip`):

XSPF Playlists

It is often desirable to have several audio clips in one player that will be played one after the other. To achieve this, we need two things: a player that is capable of doing this, and an XSPF file that contains a list of files to play.

Fortunately, there are tools available for Drupal that do this. For the player, we'll use the **JW FLV Media Player** that we've already installed. Fortunately for us, the player is able to read and play files listed in an XSPF file. For the playlist, we'll use the XSPF Playlist module.

But first, let's find out briefly just what an XSPF Playlist is.

XSPF File Format

According to Wikipedia, the XML Shareable Playlist Format is more commonly known as XSPF, and is pronounced as "spiff". The standard allows simple files to be created that can be read by any player capable of parsing the format.

As with any XML file, an XSPF file is human-readable. A sample file is shown here.
We'll be using Drupal to create files such as this:

```
<?xml version="1.0" encoding="UTF-8"?>
<playlist version="1" xmlns="http://xspf.org/ns/0/">
  <trackList>
    <track>
      <title>Rock the Casbah</title>
      <location>http://www.mysite.com/sites/mysite.com/files/music
                                  /clash/track1.mp3</location>
    </track>
    <track>
      <title>Should I Stay or Should I Go</title>
      <location>http://www.mysite.com/sites/mysite.com/files/music
                                  /clash/track2.mp3</location>
    </track>
  </trackList>
</playlist>
```

XSPF Playlist

The **XSPF Playlist** module allows you to create new playlist files by simply creating
a View of audio content. Combined with the **jQuery Media** plug-in, things fall
magically into place.

> A caveat is in order. At the time of this writing, the **XSPF Playlist** module
> was not available for Drupal 6. The module maintainer has promised
> that it will be available eventually, so the rest of this chapter is predicated
> on that happening. The examples are written as though it were already
> available, and it is expected that the techniques will not differ from what's
> presented here. However, there may be some differences by the time
> of the module's release. Please read the module's documentation if you
> experience any problems implementing it.

Install both those modules and make sure that you're using the **JW FLV Media
Player**. Also make sure that you have both **Views** and **Views UI** installed and
enabled. We'll need a content type with some audio content as well. You could
easily use the Audio node, but we're going to use the Clip content from our
previous example.

The benefit of an arrangement such as this is that we can create a View of all audio clips on our site. This could include clips associated with articles using a node reference field, and clips manually created but not referenced. These could be separate from other types of audio on the site such as a fictional **Music Clip** content type. Hopefully, you will see why we've been steering in the direction of using **FileFields** for our audio content.

Before we can use the **XSPF Playlist** module with our Views, we'll need to make some modifications to its settings page by browsing to **Administer | Site configuration | XSPF playlist settings** (at `/admin/settings/xspf_playlist`). At the time of this writing, that page is a bit clunky. Hopefully, it will be simpler soon.

Some initial settings are shown here. You can change them if desired. They should be fairly self-explanatory; in particular, you may wish to change the **Default thumbnail for playlist items** to an image on your site (as the playlist may include thumbnails for individual clips):

XSPF playlist settings

Playlist title:

> Drupal Multimedia playlist

Displayed on playlist.

Playlist info:

Information about this playlist. Some players will display this information

Default thumbnail for playlist items:

Path to your default image, requires http://mydomain.com/ . If you change this, you must save this page before the changes are available to the settings below.

File type support:

> flv,jpg,gif,png,mp3

Will only use attached files of these file types. Comma seperated list, avoid spaces.

The tricky part of configuring this module is in the next section of the page. You need to first specify what content types may be visible to the module, and next what CCK fields are fair game. Hopefully, the module will do this more automatically in the future. For now, you'll need to go through a two-step process.

First, select the **Clip** content type that we created from the list of available types, and press **Select**. (You won't see the next options until you've saved your changes.)

After submitting, you'll see a new fieldset where you'll need to select the **Audio Clip** field of the **Clip** content. As you'll see on this list, it currently lists all fields available to the system and not just the fields available to a specific type. Also make sure to check the **Use a CCK field's data** box:

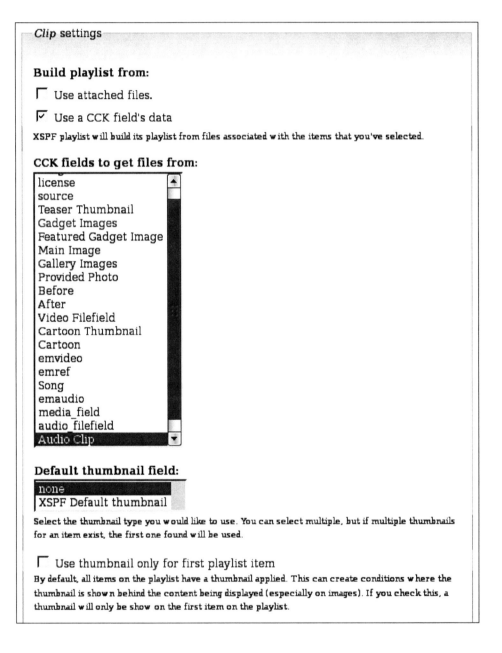

Finally, you can submit your changes and move on to the Views. If you don't configure the content type and field information properly from this screen, you'll end up with empty XSPF files and need to come back here until you get it right.

Creating Our XSPF File

Now we can build our initial file using Views. Add a View by browsing to **Administer | Site building | Views | Add** (at **admin/build/views/add**). You'll select **Node** for **View Type**, and fill in the other basic information to get things started. (We'll call ours `clips_xspf` for the **View Name**).

In our **Basic settings** section, we'll select **XSPF Playlist feed** for the **Style**. Add a **Filter** of **Node: Type**, checking the corresponding **Clip** type. Also add a **Filter** for **Node: Published** (checking the corresponding **Published** checkbox). Sort by the **Node: Post date**, **Descending**. Then add an argument, which we'll be using later, setting it to **Taxomony: Term**.

Arguments in views allow us to have a flexible URL path. In our case, we could have a URL of `clips.xspf/pop-rock` or `clips.xspf/classical`. The argument will parse whatever is after `clips.xspf` and match it to the taxonomy term. It can become quite complex, but that's outside the scope of this book:

Page: Configure Argument "Taxonomy: Term"

Title:

%1

The title to use when this argument is present; it will override the title of the view and titles from previous arguments. You can use percent substitution here to replace with argument titles. Use "%1" for the first argument, "%2" for the second, etc.

Action to take if argument is not present:

- ⦿ Display all values
- ○ Hide view / Page not found (404)
- ○ Display empty text
- ○ Summary, sorted ascending
- ○ Summary, sorted descending
- ○ Provide default argument

Wildcard:

all

If this value is received as an argument, the argument will be ignored; i.e, "all values"

Wildcard title:

All

The title to use for the wildcard in substitutions elsewhere.

Validator:

<Basic validation> ▾

Action to take if argument does not validate:

Hide view / Page not found (404) ▾

☐ Glossary mode

Glossary mode applies a limit to the number of characters used in the argument, which allows the summary view to act as a glossary.

Case:

Capitalize each word ▾

When printing the argument result, how to transform the case.

Case in path:

No transform ▾

When printing url paths, how to transform the of the argument. Do not use this unless with Postgres as it uses case sensitive comparisons.

☑ Transform spaces to dashes in URL

☐ Allow multiple arguments to work together.

If selected, multiple instances of this argument can work together, as though multiple terms were supplied to the same argument. This setting is not compatible with the "Reduce duplicates" setting.

☐ Do not display items with no value in summary

Update | Cancel | Remove

This assumes you are actually using a Taxonomy Vocabulary for your Clips. For this example, you should set up a quick vocabulary, for, say, Genre at **Administer | Content management | Taxonomy | Add vocabulary** (at `/admin/content/taxonomy/add/vocabulary`) with a few sample terms. Alternatively, you could use another argument such as **User: UID**. The rest of this will be the same regardless.

Next, add a **Page** display by pressing the **Add Display** button (with **Page** selected). Here we'll set our URL by clicking on **Path** and filling in the text field for **Page: The menu path or URL of this view**. We'll enter `clips.xspf` here.

Save your View, and you'll be able to view the raw XSPF file created by clicking **View Page** on the resulting screen. You may choose to add a term name to the end of the URL to see the taxonomy listing in action such as `http://mysite.com /clips.xspf/childrens`.

If all goes well, you'll see an XML file similar to the following. If the file is empty of nodes, you may need to review the previous section about configuring the **XSPF playlist** module:

```
<playlist version='1' xmlns='http://xspf.org/ns/0/'>
<title>Audio Clips</title>
<annotation>XSPF Playlist of Clips</annotation>
<link>http://mysite-com</link>
  <trackList>
<track>
  <creator></creator>
  <location>http://mysite-com/sites/mysite-com/files/music/childrens
                                        /track-1.mp3</location>
  <info>http://mysite-com/node/84</info>
  <type rel="mp3">mp3</type>
  <title>Twinkle, Twinkle, Little Star</title>
  <identifier>84</identifier>
</track>
  </trackList>
</playlist>
```

Building Our View

Finally, we can create a view that uses our XSPF file. We'll create another view that's nearly identical to the first, except that it creates a list of links. Then we'll embed the first view into the header of the new. And finally, we'll add some magic to the links, so they control our player. It seems like a tall order, but it should be manageable so long as we break it down into the required steps.

To create the view that will embed the XSPF file, we'll edit the original view and add a page to it. This will create a new page named **Page 1** for purposes of administration (although that can be changed), which inherits everything from the default. We'll override it as needed.

First, change the **Path** to `clips` (as opposed to `clips.xspf`), which will allow for URLs such as `http://mysite.com/clips/term-name` as we're inheriting the existing arguments from the default. Next, change the **Style** to `List`, and the **Row Style** to `Fields`. This will allow us to specify that we only display the title of a node, rather than its entire teaser. In the new **Fields** section that appears when making this change, add a **Node: Title** field, checking **Link this field to its node**. Also blank out the **Label** (which reads **Title** by default), so our title links will appear without an unnecessary label, being the only fields displayed here:

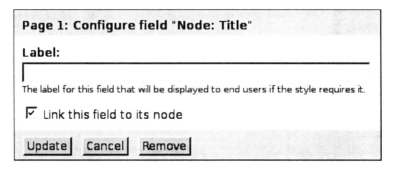

Finally, we'll have to send the XSPF file we created in the first part of this view to a player. Unfortunately, at this time, we won't be able to use jQuery Media to automatically embed our media. So we'll just manually enter the code we need.

Add a Header, making sure to press the **Override** button if it appears, as we won't use this header on the previous view. In the text area that appears, enter the following code:

```php
<?php
// change the following to reflect the actual location on your site
$player = url('mediaplayer.swf');
// this is the first view we created, using the same argument.
$xspf = url('clips.xspf/'. arg(1));
// change the width and height as desired
print "<embed
  id='clips-player'
  src='$player'
  width='400'
  height='134'
  allowscriptaccess='always'
  allowfullscreen='true'
```

```
flashvars='width=400&height=134&file=$xspf&displaywidth=140&searchb
ar=false'
/>";
?>
```

If you are using `swfobject`, you would enter the following instead, which will take care of browser compatibility:

```
<?php
// change the following to reflect the actual location on your site
$swfobject = url('swfobject.js');
// change the following to reflect the actual location on your site
$player = url('mediaplayer.swf');
// this is the first view we created, using the same argument.
$xspf = url('clips.xspf/'. arg(1));
// change width and height as desired.
print "<script type='text/javascript' src='$swfobject'></script>
<div id='player'>This text will be replaced</div>
<script type='text/javascript'>
  var so = new SWFObject('$player','clips-player','400','134','8');
  so.addParam('allowscriptaccess','always');
  so.addParam('allowfullscreen','true');
  so.addVariable('width','400');
  so.addVariable('height','134');
  so.addVariable('file','$xspf');
  so.addVariable('displaywidth','140');
  so.addVariable('searchbar','false');
  so.write('player');
</script>";
?>
```

Lastly, change the **Input format** to **PHP code**. You can now save your view, and see your results by going to a URL in the taxonomy tree such as `/clips/childrens`:

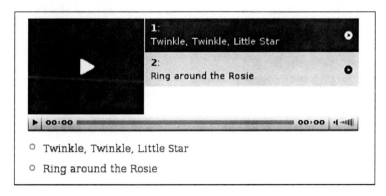

Linking Our Links

Our next task is to synchronize the links on the page with the player. Currently, if you click on them, they'll simply go to the clip's node page. We'll need to add some jQuery, alter our view, and override its theme to make this work properly.

Jeroen Wijering has written an extensive JavaScript API, which is documented at http://www.jeroenwijering.com/?item=Javascript_interaction. We'll be making use of that to build our example.

First, our player needs a unique ID and a new flashvar set so that it can receive events from JavaScript. This is what will allow our links to talk with the player. We'll need to set the `enablejs` flashvar to `True`. We also need to set the `javascriptid` flashvar to our player's ID, which is `clips-player`. If using `swfobject`, we'll add the following two lines. Otherwise, the flashvars are simply added to the flashvars screen in the embed code:

```
so.addVariable('enablejs','true');
so.addVariable('javascriptid','clips-player');
```

Next, we need to add a `click` event to our node links. This will override the behavior when a link is clicked so that rather than going to another page, it will instead send an event to our player.

Add the following to the end of the `<?php ?>` section of the view header:

```
$js = "
  // This function is required to speak with our player.
  // Don't forget the player must have a unique ID,
  // and flashvars of enablejs=true&javascriptid=the-unique-id.
  function thisMovie(swf) {
    if(navigator.appName.indexOf('Microsoft') != -1) {
      return window[swf];
    } else {
      return document[swf];
    }
  };
  if (Drupal.jsEnabled) {
    $(document).ready(function (){
      // transform the link to send events to the player.
      $('.view-content-clips .view-data-node-title a')
                                          .click(function() {
        // send the 'playitem' event to the player,
        // with the index of this node (within its jquery selection).
        // this corresponds to the same number as the playlist,
        // since the two views are both created with the same filters.
```

```
        thisMovie('clips-player').sendEvent('playitem',
        $('.view-content-clips .view-data-node-title a').index(this));
        return false;
    });
  });
}
";
drupal_add_js($js, 'inline');
```

User-Created Embeddable Playlists

Finally, we'll briefly examine the possibility for user-created playlists. Specifically, we'll take a simple idea of allowing a user to mark his or her favorite tracks, and have them appear in a playlist suitable for listening at the user's own leisure or for embedding on the user's blog.

To allow users to mark their favorite tracks, the most suitable module for the task is Flag. There are others, notably **Favorite Nodes**, and the techniques should be similar if you choose to use another option.

First, install the **Flag** module available from `http://drupal.org/project/flag`. You'll add a new bookmark from **Administer | Site building | Flags | Add** (at `/admin/build/flag/add`):

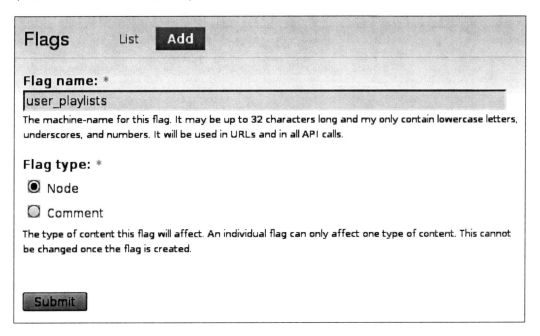

After pressing **Submit**, you'll have several text fields to configure:

Name: *

user_playlists

The machine-name for this flag. It may be up to 32 characters long and my only contain lowercase letters, underscores, and numbers. It will be used in URLs and in all API calls.

Title: *

User playlists

A short, descriptive title for this flag. It will be used in administrative interfaces to refer to this flag. Some examples could be *Bookmarks*, *Favorites*, or *Offensive*.

Flag link text: *

add to playlist

The text for the "flag this" link for this flag.

Flag link description:

Click this link to add the track to your playlist.

The description of the "flag this" link. Usually displayed on mouseover.

Flagged message:

This track has been added to your playlist.

Message displayed when the user has clicked the "flag this" link. If javascript is enabled, it will be displayed below the link. If not, it will be displayed in the message area.

Unflag link text: *

remove from playlist

The text for the "unflag this" link for this flag.

Unflag link description:

Click this link to remove the track from your playlist.

The description of the "unflag this" link. Usually displayed on mouseover.

Unflagged message:

This track has been removed from your playlist.

Message displayed when the user has clicked the "unflag this" link. If javascript is enabled, it will be displayed below the link. If not, it will be displayed in the message area.

▷   Token replacement

The **Title** is an administrative name for the flag, useful for separating this from others that might be on the site (such as favorite blog posts, stories marked for speedy deletion, and so on). We'll call this one **user_playlists**.

The **Flag Link** will appear with a clip's links, and will be what the user clicks to add a clip to his or her playlist. To make it clear, we'll enter **add to playlist** here. Likewise, the **Flag Link Description** will display a title on mouse hover, so we'll add something like **Click this link to add this track to your playlist**. The **Flagged Message** will be displayed to the user, letting him or her know the operation was successful. Just add something descriptive such as; **This track has been added to your playlist**.

Similarly, we'll add suitable descriptions for **Unflag Link**, **Unflag Link Description**, and **Unflagged Message**, which are used to remove a clip from the playlist. For this example, we'll use **remove from playlist, Click this link to remove this track from your playlist**, and **This track has been removed from your playlist**, respectively:

Roles that may use this flag: *

- ☒ authenticated user
- ☐ editor
- ☐ unverified

Checking *authenticated user* will allow all logged-in users to flag content with this flag. Anonymous users may not flag content.

- ☐ Global flag

If checked, flag is considered 'global' and each node is either flagged or not. If unchecked, each user has his or her own flag flag.

Check **authenticated user** for the **Roles that may use this flag** section. Anonymous users are not able to currently use Flags.

Finally, check the content type(s) you wish to enable for playlists. We'll just check the **Clip** node type for this example:

What nodes this bookmark may be used on: *

☐ Album

☐ Article

☐ Audio

☐ Cartoon

☑ Clip

☐ Video

Check any node types that this bookmark may be used on. You must check at least one node type.

☐ Global bookmark

If checked, bookmark is considered 'global' and each node is either marked or not. If unchecked, each user has his or her own bookmark flag.

☑ Teaser

If checked, the bookmark this link will appear on the node teasier; otherwise it will only appear on the full node view.

☐ Show on node edit form

If checked, this bookmark will appear as a checkbox on the node editing form when new nodes are created.

Submit

After submitting, each user will now be able to create his or her playlists. You will see a link that appears on the clips (and their teasers, if you checked the **Teaser** box when configuring the flag):

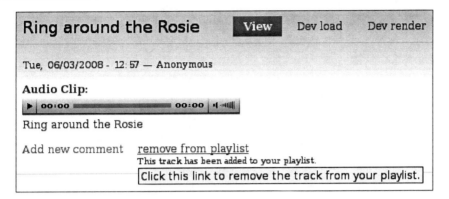

User Playlist Views

Creating a view for our custom playlists is a piece of cake, especially because we can simply build on what we've already created.

We'll clone and modify the previous view we created. To do this, go to **Administer | Site building | Views** and click on the **clone** link next to the clip_xspf view (at /admin/build/views/clone/clip_xspf). Name this **Playlist**, and click the **Next** button to make the required modifications.

Remove the **Taxonomy: Term Argument** by clicking that and then pressing **Remove**. Add a replacement argument of **Bookmarks: 'User Playlist' for UID**. You'll probably want something like %1's Playlist for the **Title**, which will replace %1 with the playlist creator's username.

For the **Page** of the view, we'll change the path from clips.xspf to playlist.xspf. Similarly, change the path of the Page 1 section of the view from clips to playlist. Finally, we'll use the PHP from the original view header, but change the $xspf variable to be url('playlist.xspf/'. arg(1).

Now if you log on, say, as user 18 and add a few favorite clips, then browse over to /playlist/18, you'll have that user's custom playlist.

Embeddable Audio

For the icing on top, we'll add a text area below the player, allowing other users to embed a user's custom player within their blog. We already have everything we need. We just need to place the player code within a text area in our View header.

When placing the player within our own page, we have access to all the JavaScript, which we won't be offering to widgets. Thus, we'll just use the straight embed code, even if we're actually using swfobject.js on our own site. We'll do that in this example. Just type the following into the View header for the playlist (Page 1) view, replacing what's there. (If you are not using swfobject.js, you'll need to adjust it accordingly, just adding the final section for the form text area.)

```php
<?php
// Change the following to reflect the actual location on your site
$swfobject = url('swfobject.js');
// Change the following to reflect the actual location on your site.
// Note that we need this to be absolute now, since we want to allow
// it to be called from other sites.
$player = url('mediaplayer.swf', array('absolute' => TRUE));
// This is the first view we created, using the same argument.
// Again we'll need an absolute path this time.
$xspf = url('playlist.xspf/'. arg(1), array('absolute' => TRUE));
// Change the width and height as desired
$width = 400;
$height = 134;
$displaywidth = 140;
// The embed code for users to paste within their own sites.
$embed = "<embed id='clips-player' src='$player' width='$width'
 height='$height' allowscriptaccess='always' allowfullscreen='true'
        flashvars='width=$width&height=$height&file=$xspf&displaywidth=
                              $displaywidth&searchbar=false' />";
// display our player on our site
print "<script type='text/javascript' src='$swfobject'></script>
<div id='player'>This text will be replaced</div>
<script type='text/javascript'>
  var so = new SWFObject('$player', 'clips-player', '$width',
                                      '$height', '8');
  so.addParam('allowscriptaccess', 'always');
  so.addParam('allowfullscreen', 'true');
  so.addVariable('width', '$width');
  so.addVariable('height', '$height');
  so.addVariable('file', '$xspf');
```

```
    so.addVariable('displaywidth', '$displaywidth');
    so.addVariable('searchbar', 'false');
    so.addVariable('enablejs', 'true');
    so.addVariable('javascriptid', 'clips-player');
    so.write('player');
</script>";
// add playlist controls to our links
$js = "
  function thisMovie(swf) {
    if(navigator.appName.indexOf('Microsoft') != -1) {
      return window[swf];
    } else {
      return document[swf];
    }
  };
  if (Drupal.jsEnabled) {
    $(document).ready(function (){
      $('.view-content-clips .view-data-node-title a').
click(function() {
        thisMovie('clips-player').sendEvent('playitem',
        $('.view-content-clips .view-data-node-title a').index(this));
        return false;
      });
    });
  }
";
drupal_add_js($js, 'inline');
// Display a text area for users to grab the embed code.
print "<div id='playlist-embed'><form><textarea name='playlist-embed'
    cols=52 rows=3>$embed</textarea><div class='description'>Copy and
        paste this code to embed the player on your own blog.</div>
                                        </form></div>";
// Display a link, and add jQuery code to toggle the textarea.
print "<div id='playlist-embed-link'><a href='#'>Embed this player on
                                        your blog</a></div>";

$js = "
  if (Drupal.jsEnabled) {
    $(document).ready(function (){
      $('#playlist-embed').hide();
      $('#playlist-embed-link a').click(function() {
        $('#playlist-embed').toggle();
        return false;
```

```
    });
  });
}
";
drupal_add_js($js, 'inline');
?>
```

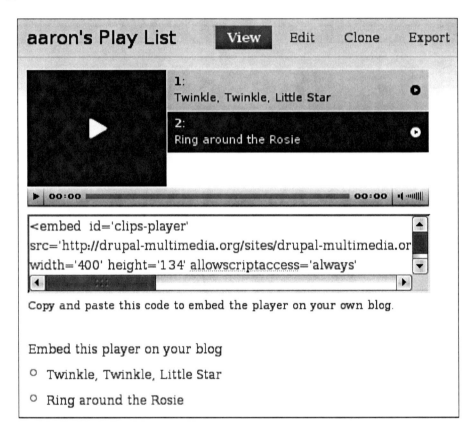

Summary

We've come a long way in this book, building on our techniques to bring them together in powerful ways. In this chapter, we've learned to combine Views and jQuery to integrate seemingly disparate sections of a page. We've interconnected audio clips with other content types and created play lists, both automatically created and user customized. Finally, we've learned how to allow users to embed players in their own sites.

11
The Future of Drupal Multimedia

What does the future hold for Drupal Multimedia? Obviously, making predictions on any subject often leads to the possibility of future embarrassment for the author, when the predictions inevitably are underestimated or over-exaggerated. Still, they are fun to make.

To make this relevant, I, as an author shall attempt for the most part to stay with the possible near future. Some of these items are fairly certain, and may already be in place by the time you read this, such as the introduction of `hook_file` in the core. Others are more speculative. Though seemingly inevitable at the time of writing, new efforts and technologies could easily change their direction or introduce new revolutionary ideas.

File Handling

First, let's examine the nuts and bolts of an exciting change right around the corner. A long-time dream of developers and administrators of Drupal is the better support for multimedia in the core. As every excited newcomer to Drupal has quickly learned, there is currently no built-in way to handle even simply adding images to a site. Thus, the need for this book.

This is soon to change. For over a year, there has been an exciting issue in the Drupal project queue titled "*Add hook_file and make files into a 1st class Drupal object*" (available at `http://drupal.org/node/142995`). Slated for Drupal 7, this addition will revolutionize media handling for developers by providing a simple `hook_file` to the mix. This will allow modules to act on changes to the file system so that they can insert their own functions when a file is added, deleted, loaded, and so on.

Why This Is Profound

Files in Drupal have a long history of being the evil step-children of nodes. Until the release of Drupal 6, they were inextricably tied to nodes at the database level. However, they were finally set free, allowing for some new uses for files, some of which have yet to be realized. (As an example, with **Views 2** you can now create a view listing of files.)

Still, it's difficult to act directly on files. The API for uploading and manipulating files is crude and doesn't allow for modules to act on events. The proposed patch for `hook_file` on the fast track for adoption in Drupal 7 will create several new operational hooks, allowing modules to act on a file when it's uploaded, copied, moved, loaded, deleted, and more.

This functionality will allow modules to work in tandem with a more unified approach. Rather than a dozen modules needlessly duplicating code just to display thumbnails or add watermarks, and sometimes still missing the mark, developers will be able to act on file operations to create new engines that affect all image files, regardless of the source.

This brings us to Multimedia APIs.

Multimedia APIs

Once we have a File API in place, I believe we'll witness a transformation in multimedia handling in Drupal. Developers will create just a handful of multimedia engines that can be used to power features such as UI and asset handling. Additionally, adding new functionality should be easier, as a developer interested in creating a new way to visualize data won't have to worry about how that data gets there in the first place.

We already have hints of this. **FileField** is showing the way by offering a unified file upload system with one module that is suitable for helper modules to determine how to handle the data. Already, we can use this to simplify audio, video, and image handling, when those modules make use of **FileField** as a base API (as **ImageField** already does).

Finally, the experimental **Transformer** module hints at more possibilities, although still in its infancy. It promises to be what **ImageCache** is for all types of media, for instance by creating audio clips or cropping video. That module still has a long way to go, but once `hook_file` is in the core, it won't be long before the **Transformer** module or some other steps up to offer that functionality.

Multimedia in the Core

The next step, of course, will be to put multimedia handling in the core. Over three years ago, the **Image** module was the most-downloaded contributed module for Drupal. Though the demand for its functionality is high, it is still not in the core.

One of the stated reasons for not supporting multimedia as a core feature has been to allow various methods to compete in "the wild of contrib". This has been a good thing for the most part as several modules and approaches have fallen by the wayside, while others, unforeseen a couple of years ago, have quickly risen to the top.

This state will soon change for the better. Dries Buytaert (`http://buytaert.net/`) has reiterated on several recent occasions the need, spoken across the board by developers and end users, for better media handling within Drupal. The developers are rising to the task. For instance, there is a well-received proposal to merge **Image** with **ImageField**, the current two contenders for core image handling.

However, before this could happen, parts of CCK and Views will also need to make it into the core. All of this is in discussion and deliberation, and is a large undertaking. Fortunately for all of us, this very task is currently in process.

Of course, a new module could easily rise to the forefront, given the organic nature of open source development. **FileField** may ultimately end up unifying all the media modules. Or a new method of asset management may become popular. After `hook_file` and CCK fields are in core, it is likely that **FileField** (or its like) will also find its way there.

The Internet itself may also evolve, especially as distributed utility file services such as Amazon S3, Nirvanix, and Ourmedia are being heavily used. We've already seen this happen with video, as discussed earlier in this book.

This points back to the wisdom of being conservative with the core. Things happen quickly in Drupal, but it takes time for the effects to reverberate through the community.

Multipurpose Fields

Drupal has definitely matured and I believe that its developers are entering a period of introspection. This includes an eye towards unifying media APIs and reducing the difficulty for the end users of their modules. It is also entering an exciting time of collaboration, not just with the core of Drupal, but also in contributed modules.

As the developer and co-maintainer of the **Embedded Media Field**, one of the more frequent requests I have heard is to create an all-in-one media content field that can parse external video, audio, and images, at the same time allowing the upload and display of user-submitted media. I suspect other developers have fielded the same requests, which have been a part of the move over the past year or so to create unified approaches such as with **Media Mover**, **Asset**, **Embedded Media Field**, **FileField**, and so on.

Although it might be easy to dismiss that, there's actually no technical reason not to allow this. Due to some limitations of the browsers, there would be some (simple) problems to solve, namely with the UI since for security purposes, an upload field is handled differently than the simple text field used to paste a YouTube video URL. Additionally, there were some inherent limitations in CCK during Drupal 5 that would have made this a difficult request to fulfill.

However, there are new hooks in place for CCK in Drupal 6 that should make this kind of feature easier to achieve. In fact, there has been some discussion about allowing many disparate types of fields to share the same user space.

Whether this will happen through one module, one suite of modules, or with a unifying API in core is yet to be seen. However, I expect that by the time this book is updated for Drupal 7, there should be at least one solution to this request.

Image versus ImageField

One of the big questions many new developers struggle over is whether to use the **Image** module or **ImageField**. Fortunately, this debate may soon end, particularly as hook_file becomes a reality and more of CCK fields find their way in core. With better multimedia file handling that is a core feature of Drupal, modules such as these will be able to strip out the repeated functionality of things such as file uploading and image handling, and concentrate on user interface.

There have been discussions to merge the two modules, so that they both use the mechanics of **ImageField**, which is in turn already dependent on **FileField**. In this case, the **ImageField** module would probably become deprecated in favor of the **Image** namespace.

In order to make this transition complete, we would require a migration path to ensure that there is an API for the existing modules depending on current functionality of the **Image** module. There is already a script to handle this, developed by Moshe Weitzman at http://drupal.org/node/201983#comment-880481. The next step is to ensure that the **Image** module's API is supported by the **ImageField** functionality.

Similarly, the **Audio** and deprecated **Video** modules will probably convert their node types to also depend on **FileField**.

The developers of these modules have been actively involved in conversations and planning towards making this happen.

Content Field is King

The old adage, content is king, continues to hold true in Drupal. Traditionally, this has meant the node is king. However, with the advent of CCK, we have seen a shift to the content field. Functionality that was once the domain of the node has become increasingly fragmented, allowing for the mix and mash currently dominating Drupal. Thus, instead of separate types for blogs, images, and audio, we can combine them as we please, creating new node types on the fly to suit specific purposes.

This trend will certainly continue, mirroring the trend on the Internet to fragment our data. We will increasingly need to have content within our site, so that it will be discovered regardless of what node it's connected to, or whether it's even connected to a node.

As we've discussed, this has already begun to happen. For instance, files are no longer connected to nodes in the database. Additionally, the **Node Reference** field allows nodes to be detached from the original source, so they may be, as well, part of another node. As we practiced in earlier chapters, this allows us to create, for instance, images, video, and audio clips that may be referenced within various nodes and galleries, so that the original node is not even accessed individually anymore.

Eventually, what we may find is that it is no longer necessary or wanted to tie data on our site to a specific node. Rather, we may have it further fragmented into individual fields, which can be mixed and referenced as necessary within nodes.

Core Fields

As we discussed earlier, another exciting development for Drupal is the addition of CCK fields into the core, for Drupal 7. Core developers have been actively stripping the base engine from the module into Drupal, separating the API from the UI. The field storage engine, field creation API, and basic field definitions will be part of the standard Drupal offering, while an administration UI to create new fields will remain as a contributed module.

As we know, **ImageField** is already dependent on **FileField**, and with the combination of `hook_file` and the API for that module, we'll be quickly on our way to a unified method of file handling, freeing developers to focus more strongly on innovation in UI and display, rather than constantly reinventing the wheel.

Bringing this back to the **Image** versus **ImageField** discussion, this means that the **Image** module will be able to move its image functionality to a field, automatically creating (and converting) a field to handle images. This would not depend on CCK, although it would be exposed to CCK's UI, as it will simply use the core field engine to do this work.

User Experience

Although Drupal can be quite flashy for the end user, as evidenced by how quickly it is being adopted by corporate sites, it is certainly lacking for the administrators and editors. Even trying to decide one from among the dozens of contending multimedia modules to install for a particular need is difficult enough. Trying to navigate the slush of administration pages and often poor or non-existent documentation is a nightmare.

This needs to change.

Administration Interface

When modules are first introduced, they are generally to scratch an itch, to create a feature for the end user, often sponsored by a client who has a specific need. As the modules mature, their developers tend to put a little more thought than initially towards making configuration easier. Sometimes this is due to personal experience, or by the inspiration of other modules. Often, it's simply to try to keep support requests in the issue queues down.

Raising the bar for module developers, **Views 2** and **Panels 2** have become much easier for configuration than they had been previously. Rather than an unbearably long page of collapsible fieldsets that sometimes obscured important information, the new configuration pages for these modules are far more intuitive. They not only pack all the information into one area using a combination of tabs and drawers to load information dynamically as needed, but the form elements are well-documented on screen with additional detailed help available as pop-ups when combined with the **Advanced Help** module.

As we also saw in earlier chapters, the **Asset** module in addition to other similar modules, already makes file management easier. Once hook_file is in place, relieving the strain on multimedia handling modules, modules such as **Asset** can concentrate on UI. Then users can choose which "flavor" to install, and be assured that they all use the same solid engine beneath.

Similarly, when fields (and hopefully a views-like API) are in core, developers may decide to create competing administrative interfaces to access and control their functionality. This competition will ensure we're constantly striving towards the best, and allow administrators and developers to confidently experiment, knowing the underlying data will be preserved between implementations.

Usability Testing

Several universities have been partnering with the Drupal community, including the University of Minnesota and the University of Baltimore. Besides observing the obvious dissonance between the intent of many module developers and the ensuing confusion of the editors, these studies are also offering new solutions.

Additionally, there is a current Google Summer of Code project to help address this, the **Usability Test Suite**, which came directly from a major study conducted at UMN earlier this year.

Testing needs to continue in order to help Drupal pass the hurdle of its perceived difficult learning curve and unfriendliness to new administrators. Additionally, attention needs to be given to the interfaces involving multimedia so that solutions such as the **Asset** module already offers become expected, making administration of multimedia and file management easier and more intuitive than it currently is.

Embeddable Widgets

I am personally quite excited about the future of embeddable widgets, and have blogged about it on various occasions at `http://aaronwinborn.com/`. As stated in Chapter 11, I believe that as the **Embed Widgets** module matures, it will transform how Drupal integrates with the rest of the Internet.

We are already seeing a push towards distributed data, as seen with sites such as Flickr, YouTube, and Google Docs. I believe that is just the tip of the iceberg.

At Advomatic over the past year, I have already seen an increase of clients requesting embeddable widgets, and have implemented a number of them myself. Each has been custom crafted, a process that will become significantly easier in the near future.

This will just continue to escalate. Widgets are becoming increasingly in demand on the Internet in general, and Drupal is rising to the challenge. Widgets themselves are beginning to be seen as mini-sites, no longer tied to a page or a site or even a URL.

A site that is able to fragment into a million pieces, and yet is able to maintain its identity as it integrates into a larger and possibly unrelated page or blog post will be a site that will thrive in the multi-faceted demands and marvels of the new Internet.

The current challenge is to allow the easy creation of widgets, both administratively and by end users. For instance, besides the familiar embeddable videos that have exploded around the Internet since the advent of YouTube, sites increasingly want to create mash-ups of media such as multimedia slideshows.

As we explored in earlier chapters, Drupal already allows for the easy creation of user-created audio and video playlists, which in turn can easily be turned into widgets with the **Embed Widgets** module. Innovation on this and similar fronts should be led by Drupal developers as more sites demand it.

Semantic Multimedia

As widgets will create new external demands on sites, so too will data organization create new internal demands.

The concept of a Semantic Web as envisioned by Tim Berners-Lee (http://www.w3.org/People/Berners-Lee/), the inventor of the World Wide Web, is meant to be a way to organize and collect data by its underlying meaning. It may be fully possible in the not-so-distant future to verbally speak with the Internet and retrieve the desired information. As stepping stones towards this vision, we already are able to tag content using taxonomy and keywords. The Semantic Web allows us, for instance, to make connections between the data to offer more meaningful results to users' search queries.

Semantic Multimedia is a subset of the work in progress towards creating a Semantic Web. Still in its infancy, developers interested in ensuring that multimedia are embraced by the emerging Semantic Web should put effort into tagging media at both the high level of taxonomy and at lower levels such as by utilizing the **getID3** module. Meanwhile, technology will continue to improve, allowing at least automatic extraction in the future of a media file's volume, pitch, colors, and someday perhaps even spoken text.

Development has been active for years on helping to realize a Semantic Web, particularly with textual content. However, much still has to happen to draw multimedia content into the semantic fold. It is not enough for hardware and bandwidth to improve for delivery of multimedia. More effort needs to be put into automatically creating and even extracting low-level descriptors of that content so that it can be linked and retrieved more intelligently.

Fortunately, there are simple things we can already do in Drupal to ensure we're ready for Web 3.0. By understanding the concepts behind Semantic Multimedia, we can ensure we're using tags with our data that sufficiently describe it.

Microformats

Microformats are a way to organize data. Using HTML tags or XML markup, it is possible to describe data so that it can be discovered easily by other applications.

For instance, an HTML link to a video might normally read `<a href="http://example.com/video.mpg">My Video</a>`. Even without creating new microformats and only using existing tags, we could change that to read `<a href="http://example.com/video.mpg" title="Playing Jump Rope in the Park" type="video/mpeg" hreflang="en-US">My Video</a>`. This would reference the title, content type, and language in the link. There are other existing uses here as well, such as using the otherwise deprecated `urn` attribute to use a unique identifier to relate videos of various formats to each other, as described by Charles Iliya Krempeaux at `http://changelog.ca/log/2005/10/16/thoughts_on_video_and_audio_microformats`.

RDF Triples

There are several efforts in place to help realize the visions for a Semantic Web. Among the more developed and currently embraced by many Drupal developers is Resource Description Framework or RDF.

RDF is a specification for data organization that uses so-called "triples" to describe information. For instance, the concept of "Monarch Butterflies migrate to and from Mexico" could be expressed with a subject, "Monarch Butterflies", a verb "to migrate", and an object "to and from Mexico". With its linguistic roots, it should be intuitive to human understanding, allowing for easy access and combination of data.

There is a slow but growing move to convert data into RDF. Some of this can happen automatically with the help of text, and there is already an RDF contributed module available for Drupal, with talk of putting some of this functionality into the core.

Tagging Semantic Multimedia

The current state of technology requires audio and video to be tagged before it can become part of the Semantic Web, although there are projects in the works such as by Google and by some universities to overcome the current limitations involved in doing this automatically.

However, it is certainly possible to manually expose high-level media data. Notably, Drupal handles this well with taxonomy. Additionally, using such modules as GetID3, it is possible to expose further information about a media clip within the file. Finally, using additional CCK text fields is another easy way for editors to mark attached data with multimedia.

Whether RDF, microformats, or some combination will become a defacto standard for Drupal is yet to be seen. However, the sooner this concept is embraced, especially for multimedia, the more prepared Drupal will be to continue to lead the way for the rest.

Mobile Web

A growing proportion of the Web access on the Internet is from mobile web browsers. This includes PPCs such as Blackberry and mobile phones such as the iPhone. It is becoming increasingly important that we support these formats, as more people begin using mobile technology to access the Internet.

In many cases, we don't need to do too much more to support them. The manufacturers of most mobile computers and phones do their best to support standard markup and CSS, so that Drupal sites will work fine out of the box. When theming, we probably won't go too wrong as long as we adhere to web standards.

However, there are sometimes design considerations that must be taken into account when creating a site. For instance, though many sites use a sidebar for navigation, it is more convenient for most mobile users to have a navigation bar at the top of the screen. Also, due to the small size of most mobile screens, it is usually easier to read content in a single column, rather than several columns as many modern sites use.

To cater to these needs, it is possible to create a new stylesheet that better supports mobile technology such as iPhones. This stylesheet will be loaded conditionally by the browser in question. We'll just add a new stylesheet with a simple call to Drupal for our theme: `drupal_add_css(path_to_theme() . '/handheld.css', 'theme', 'handheld')`. See `http://www.w3.org/TR/REC-CSS2/media.html` for more information on stylesheets for various devices.

New Media

A discussion about the future of multimedia would not be complete without a foray into new types of media. Even recently, this would have seemed entirely in the realm of speculative science fiction. Now, however, we can actually see this in our own living rooms.

Although this last section is highly speculative, it is important to remember that changes can happen quickly on the Internet and within Drupal. For instance, YouTube didn't exist before 2005, and it opened a new model for embedding third-party videos that Drupal quickly embraced.

Virtual Reality

Humans have literally dreamed about virtual reality for probably their entire existence. Every night, each of us enters a simulated reality that competes with the world we experience during our waking state. The Taoist philosopher Zhuangzi, in a well-known musing, dreamed once that he was a butterfly. Upon waking, he wondered if it were he that dreamed of being a butterfly or if he were the butterfly dreaming of being Zhuangzi.

Though it seems a pipe dream to build a simulated reality that can even approach the level of detail present in our nightly dreams, let alone that of waking reality, there are signs that we may fast be approaching that.

And what would that portend for the Web as we rush ahead through the decades?

Second Life

Linden Lab's Second Life is a well-known example of a virtual world, where users are able to freely move in a simulated 3D space. Additionally, the interface is a portal to the Web so that walking or flying to an area and clicking can bring up a relevant web page.

This type of interface with the Internet is a portent for possibly the near future. Currently, web browsers are limited to the two-dimensional page for which a site's nodes are generally designed. Using Flash and other methods, we can already see what navigation may be like with the added dimension of depth. And as bandwidth increases and browser technology improves, users will clamor for 3D.

When that time comes, Drupal will already be primed to dominate the market as its inevitable adoption of RDF triples and the Semantic Web should be well-suited for describing a three-dimensional environment. And many Drupal themers already develop for browsing within Second Life without even knowing it. It uses Mozilla to serve web pages.

Tactile Media

In *Drupal Multimedia*, we covered the senses of sight and sound fairly comprehensively. In a few short years, I expect that an update to this book would require a section on tactile media as well.

The feedback of touch will be an important development for navigation through the Web, particularly as it becomes more three dimensional. In fact, by the time we are able to immerse ourselves in such an artificial environment, possibly more people who are connected to that Internet may choose to spend more waking time there than in the physical world. Whether that is a good or bad thing is a value judgment that I will not make here. I'm simply a messenger.

Though the field is still in its infancy, there are several mature products already available that help to simulate the sense of touch. Some of them are already in millions of households around the world.

Wii

The Wii Remote controller is famous for its ability to sense motion when interfacing with the Wii game console. Obviously, that technology should be useful for navigating through a three-dimensional environment. However, that relates to Drupal about as much as a mouse wheel does.

The more exciting piece, where Drupal will have a role, is in a less discussed feature of the controller, its rumble functionality.

Of course, this is not new, and has been present in computer game controllers for years. Still this is tactile feedback, albeit a crude example. By the time the Web has embraced 3D, the need for at least crude tactile feedback will present itself, if it hasn't already, and controllers like the Wii Remote will probably dominate the early markets.

Thus, the Drupal node of the future may contain fields for "touch files", to tactilely indicate a button to press, to rumble an access denied warning, or even to simulate stroking a purring cat. (And like the example of Second Life, themers already develop for the Wii when they develop for the Opera web browser.)

Embedded Smell Field?

Although this might seem like a joke, the concept of embedding media that stimulates our sense of smell and even taste is no laughing matter. Advertisers have long known the power of our olfactory senses, as our olfactory nerve is a hot-wire directly into our brain. Indeed, smell is tied to our most primal memories. Even reading about the scent of freshly-baked bread or a random whiff of honeysuckle in the park can evoke strong childhood memories.

Packaging in the store is regularly scented. Probably millions of dollars a year are spent in research for artificial smell and taste. Once the remote transmission of chemical olfactory footprints is perfected, corporations will be able to invade our homes directly with ads filled with enticing scents and pheromones, and we'll happily enable them. Fortunately, there will be less commercial uses as well: Imagine embedding the scent of a flower with its photograph on a site such as Flickr.

After all, once we can play World of Warcraft and smell the pungent odors of the swamp as an Orcish foot soldier, or literally taste the ozone from that wizard's lightening bolt, we'll never want to go back.

Summary

In this chapter, we have taken a close look at Drupal in the months ahead, and a far look at the future of multimedia and what it means for Drupal developers, editors, and administrators.

File handling and multimedia APIs are right on the horizon, and will spur module development, paving the way for multimedia handling in the core. As Drupal is becoming more user-centric, developers are listening to the gripes of editors and administrators, making the system easier for everyone to use. Embeddable widgets will revolutionize Drupal, and combined with RDF and Microformat support, Drupal will continue to be King (and Queen!) of Content Management on the Web.

In the years or decades following, we'll continue to see advances on media on the Internet such as 3D display and navigation and tactile feedback. Although these may seem far-fetched to many readers, innovation is being realized daily on all those fronts, and it may here be sooner than many of us realize. By that time Drupal may well be the definer of standards, as its developers, old and new, continue to learn and grow with the field.

This book is but a snapshot of the current state of Drupal Multimedia, and I hope it is comprehensive and profoundly useful to its readers. You are encouraged to visit `http://drupalmultimedia.org/` for more up-to-date information, and to read my blog at `http://aaronwinborn.com/` for my other Drupal interests.

As emphasized throughout this book, you are also strongly encouraged to give back to the community as your knowledge of Drupal and multimedia grows. If you find a bug, jump into a module's issue queue! If you're able to fix the code, then submit a patch. But even if you don't program, reviewing or testing a patch can speed along development, and garner praise and kudos from the Drupal community!

Index

Image Credits

A book like Drupal Multimedia requires more than simple screen shots for its demonstrations. The author created all of the screen shots throughout the book. However, many images were used from the Creative Commons and Public Domain to illustrate certain techniques. These are listed here, with their sources and licenses as available.

Works released under the Creative Commons Attribution (by) license may be distributed, remixed, tweaked, and built upon, even commercially, as long as they credit the original creator.

Works released under the Creative Commons Attribution-Share Alike license (by-sa) may be distributed, remixed, tweaked, and built upon, even commercially, as long as they credit the original creator and are licensed under the identical terms.

More information about the Creative Commons Attribution and Attribution-Share Alike licenses, including the complete legal code, can be found at http://creativecommons.org/about/licenses.

Chapter 2:

Baskets Four Styles, by Jeremy Kemp, Public Domain, at http://en.wikipedia.org/wiki/Image:Baskets_four_styles.jpg.

Redrood River, by Arnold Kramer, Creative Commons Attribution, at http://en.wikipedia.org/wiki/Image:Redwood_River_800x569.jpg.

***, by Andrzej G, Creative Commons Attribution-Share Alike, at http://openphoto.net/gallery/image.html?image_id=8262&hints

Mary and Child, by Mylene Bressan, Creative Commons Attribution, at http://openphoto.net/gallery/image.html?image_id=9488&hints=sculpture_mary_child.

Aurora borealis seen from space aboard Space Shuttle Atlantis during STS-117 mission, NASA, Public Domain.

Robot Asimo Cropped, by Flickr user 'xcaballe', Creative Commons Attribution-Share Alike, at http://www.flickr.com/photos/xcaballe/13403082/.

Asimo Look: New Design, by Flickr user 'AZAdam', Creative Commons Attribution-Share Alike, at http://www.flickr.com/photos/38074672@N00/83278753/.

Zebra in South Africa, Photo by Lukas Kaffer, Creative Commons Attribution, at http://en.wikipedia.org/wiki/Image:Beautiful_Zebra_in_South_Africa.JPG.

Chapter 3:

Monkey Typing, Visual by www.PDImages.com, Creative Commons Attribution, at http://www.pdimages.com/00812.html-ssi.

Edison Mimeograph and Electric Pen, Edison National Historic Site, Public Domain, at http://www.nps.gov/archive/edis/edisonia/graphics/09000001.jpg.

Edison electric pen and press, Edison National Historic Site, Public Domain, at
http://www.nps.gov/archive/edis/edisonia/graphics/09100000.jpg.

Astronaut in Space, NASA, Public Domain, at http://grin.hq.nasa.gov/ABSTRACTS/
GPN-2000-001156.html.

Grouper/Gorgone, by Albert Kok, Public Domain, at http://commons.wikimedia.org/
wiki/Image:Grouper_gorgone.JPG.

Goliath Grouper, by Clinton & Charles Robertson, Public Domain, at
http://www.flickr.com/photos/20087733@N00/411049510/.

Blue Spotted Grouper, by Adrian Pingstone, Public Domain, at
http://commons.wikimedia.org/wiki/Image:Blue-spotted.grouper.arp.jpg.

Giant Grouper, by Wikimedia user Diliff, Creative Commons Attribution, at http://
commons.wikimedia.org/wiki/Image:Georgia_Aquarium_-_Giant_Grouper.jpg.

Neutron Star, NASA, Public Domain.

Rutherford Birchard Hayes, Library of Congress Prints and Photographs Division, Public
Domain, at http://hdl.loc.gov/loc.pnp/cwpbh.03606.

Martin Van Buren, Library of Congress Prints and Photographs Division. Brady-Handy
Photograph Collection, Public Domain, at http://hdl.loc.gov/loc.pnp/cwpbh.03542.

Millard Fillmore, Library of Congress Prints and Photographs Division. Brady-Handy
Photograph Collection, Public Domain, at http://hdl.loc.gov/loc.pnp/cwpbh.00699.

Europe 2002 – Circus Stamp FO 415 of the Faroe Islands, Artist: Anna Katrina Olsen (aged 13),
Postverk Føroya - Philatelic Office, Public Domain, at http://commons.wikimedia.org/
wiki/Image:Faroe_stamp_415_clowns.jpg.

Chapter 4

The Meteorologists, Erik Gecas, used by permission of the artist, at
http://erikgecas.com/node/25.

Chapter 6

Still frame from the animated cartoon "Little Swee' Pea" (1936), Public Domain.

Chapter 7

Sleeping Hog, by Flickr user 'noahg.', Creative Commons Attribution, at
http://www.flickr.com/photos/noahbulgaria/270090287/.

Screenshot of Kaltura's platform, Kaltura, used by permission, at http://kaltura.com/.

Chapter 10

Screenshot of Air America's "Listen" media player, Air America, used by permission, at
http://airamerica.com/listen.

Packt Open Source Project Royalties

When we sell a book written on an Open Source project, we pay a royalty directly to that project. Therefore by purchasing Drupal Multimedia, Packt will have given some of the money received to the Drupal Project.

In the long term, we see ourselves and you—customers and readers of our books—as part of the Open Source ecosystem, providing sustainable revenue for the projects we publish on. Our aim at Packt is to establish publishing royalties as an essential part of the service and support a business model that sustains Open Source.

If you're working with an Open Source project that you would like us to publish on, and subsequently pay royalties to, please get in touch with us.

Writing for Packt

We welcome all inquiries from people who are interested in authoring. Book proposals should be sent to author@packtpub.com. If your book idea is still at an early stage and you would like to discuss it first before writing a formal book proposal, contact us; one of our commissioning editors will get in touch with you.

We're not just looking for published authors; if you have strong technical skills but no writing experience, our experienced editors can help you develop a writing career, or simply get some additional reward for your expertise.

About Packt Publishing

Packt, pronounced 'packed', published its first book "Mastering phpMyAdmin for Effective MySQL Management" in April 2004 and subsequently continued to specialize in publishing highly focused books on specific technologies and solutions.

Our books and publications share the experiences of your fellow IT professionals in adapting and customizing today's systems, applications, and frameworks. Our solution-based books give you the knowledge and power to customize the software and technologies you're using to get the job done. Packt books are more specific and less general than the IT books you have seen in the past. Our unique business model allows us to bring you more focused information, giving you more of what you need to know, and less of what you don't.

Packt is a modern, yet unique publishing company, which focuses on producing quality, cutting-edge books for communities of developers, administrators, and newbies alike. For more information, please visit our website: www.PacktPub.com.

Building Powerful and Robust Websites with Drupal 6

ISBN: 978-1-847192-97-4   Paperback: 362 pages

Build your own professional blog, forum, portal or community website with Drupal 6

1. Set up, configure, and deploy Drupal 6

2. Harness Drupal's world-class Content Management System

3. Design and implement your website's look and feel

4. Easily add exciting and powerful features

5. Promote, manage, and maintain your live website

Drupal 6 Themes

ISBN: 978-1-847195-66-1   Paperback: 291 pages

Create new themes for your Drupal 6 site with clean layout and powerful CSS styling

1. Learn to create new Drupal 6 themes

2. No experience of Drupal theming required

3. Techniques and tools for creating and modifying themes

4. A complete guide to the system's themable elements

Please check **www.PacktPub.com** for information on our titles

Printed in the United Kingdom by
Lightning Source UK Ltd., Milton Keynes
139686UK00001B/70/P